CW01304422

# The Kingdom of Heaven within The Holy Book of the Great Invisible Spirit ☺

### A Spiritual Transformation

*"Again, the kingdom of heaven is like unto treasure hid in a field; the which when a man hath found, he hideth, and for joy thereof goeth and selleth all that he hath, and buyeth that field."*
**Matthew 13:44**

*by*
*Sanetha*™

**BALBOA.**
PRESS
A DIVISION OF HAY HOUSE

*Copyright © 2012 by Annette Renee Moreland (Sanetha).*

*All rights reserved. No part of this book may be used or reproduced by any means, graphic, electronic, or mechanical, including photocopying, recording, taping or by any information storage retrieval system without the written permission of the publisher except in the case of brief quotations embodied in critical articles and reviews.*

*Balboa Press books may be ordered through booksellers or by contacting:*

*Balboa Press
A Division of Hay House
1663 Liberty Drive
Bloomington, IN 47403
www.balboapress.com
1-(877) 407-4847*

*Because of the dynamic nature of the Internet, any web addresses or links contained in this book may have changed since publication and may no longer be valid. The views expressed in this work are solely those of the author and do not necessarily reflect the views of the publisher, and the publisher hereby disclaims any responsibility for them.*

*The author of this book does not dispense medical advice or prescribe the use of any technique as a form of treatment for physical, emotional, or medical problems without the advice of a physician, either directly or indirectly. The intent of the author is only to offer information of a general nature to help you in your quest for emotional and spiritual well-being. In the event you use any of the information in this book for yourself, which is your constitutional right, the author and publisher assume no responsibility for your actions.*

*Any people depicted in stock imagery provided by Thinkstock are models, and such images are being used for illustrative purposes only.
Certain stock imagery © Thinkstock.*

*ISBN: 978-1-4525-5038-1 (sc)
ISBN: 978-1-4525-5040-4 (hc)
ISBN: 978-1-4525-5039-8 (e)*

*Library of Congress Control Number: 2012912521*

*Printed in the United States of America*

*Balboa Press rev. date: 07/27/2012*

THE KINGDOM OF HEAVEN within THE HOLY BOOK of THE GREAT INVISIBLE SPIRIT☺

is a magnificent tribute to all the Lightworkers who have searched throughout eternity for the greater truths of the universe. Who are you? What are you here to do? What can we contribute to our fellow man and the beautiful planet? This book shines the light upon our origins, our primordial lifetimes, and all the different parts of ourselves that unite us with our soul family throughout our history here on Earth and beyond.

Sanetha is an inspiration as she explores the realms within the heart, mind, and soul, in search of the answers. Beautifully and brilliantly written, this work unlocks ideas and conscious energy that have been hidden, sometimes in plain sight. You will find as you read these words more of your soul comes alive and awakened. There is an energetic blessing and transformation unfurled in each section of this book that enlivens every molecule of your being as you read each page. This energy, as it connected with my being, triggered a remembrance of the joy, love, and eternal youth that I had locked within me, and I found that I could hardly put this book down. It is highly recommended to read over and over as each time more can become awakened for you.

It is with our deepest gratitude and sincere blessing that we dedicate this book to our fellow brother and sister Lightworkers and Seekers of Consciousness. May your path be filled with gratitude, love and joy as well.

Love, Gratitude & Blessings,
Vanessa Riyasat, The Angelic Council, and The Masters of Light

Annette Moreland's (aka Sanetha's) book *THE KINGDOM OF HEAVEN within THE HOLY BOOK of THE GREAT INVISIBLE SPIRIT*☺ offers an insightful look at the meaning of our journey here in this life, as well as enlightening revelations on what (and who) we bring with us from our past lives. This accessible and compelling book mixes stories of its author's personal experiences in this and past lives with profound yet logical wisdom from the author's higher self, Sanetha, on the amazing power we all hold at the very core of our DNA. Additionally, a generous helping of traditional Bible stories from the King James version are cited throughout, lending age-old validation and context to the New Age concepts explored in the book. In sum, *THE KINGDOM OF HEAVEN within THE HOLY BOOK of THE GREAT INVISIBLE SPIRIT*☺ provides a thorough and essential message for all of us to hear again and again: God is in all of us and we are here to realize the divine plan we created long ago. We can do so by exerting our free will to spread love and light in all that we do, forever listening to our God-spark within.—Dawne Brooks, editor

# Contents

| | | |
|---|---|---|
| *PART I* | *SOULY TRUTH* | 1 |
| INTRODUCTION | THE TIME IS NOW! | 3 |
| CHAPTER I | THE TRUTH WILL SET YOU FREE | 9 |
| | ADAM & EVE, NOT THE FIRST ON EARTH | 9 |
| | SETH | 11 |
| | WHO AM I? | 13 |
| | WE ARE ONE | 15 |
| | LOVE CONQUERS ALL—THE DOORS OPEN | 17 |
| | THE SEARCH FOR THE HOLY GRAIL | 20 |
| | THE GREAT INVISIBLE SPIRIT | 20 |
| CHAPTER II | THE GREAT BROTHERHOOD OF LIGHT | 22 |
| | A COSMIC CYCLE | 22 |
| | SOME ROSES STINK AND SOME SKUNKS SMELL PRETTY | 23 |
| | PAY ATTENTION! TIME TO WAKE UP! | 24 |
| | MULTIPLE LIFETIMES | 26 |
| | THERE ARE NO MISTAKES | 26 |
| CHAPTER III | AS ABOVE, SO BELOW | 28 |
| | FINDING YOUR SOUL PURPOSE | 28 |
| | THE SHIFT—3D TO 5D | 29 |
| | NO FEAR—FEAR FEEDS MORE FEAR | 29 |
| | THE TIME OF THE END—NOT THE END OF TIME | 30 |
| | THE TIME OF THE END | 31 |

AGE OF AQUARIUS ... 33
2012—REBOOTING THE SYSTEM ... 33

## PART II  SPIRITS NEVER DIE ... 43

### CHAPTER I  LOVE, LOVE, LOVE ... 45

UNIVERSAL LAWS ... 45
LOSING LOVED ONES—MORE THAN MEETS THE EYES ... 47
MICHAEL'S GIFT—GIFT IT FORWARD ☺ ... 48
THERE ARE NO COINCIDENCES ... 51
THE SOUL KNOWS ... 55
THE ANGELS CAME—THE ROOM FILLED WITH A
   GLORIOUS LIGHT ... 57
I AM ... 60
REACHING FOR THE STARS ... 61
SPIRITUAL BEINGS ... 62

### CHAPTER II  OLD SOULS ... 65

ELIJAH ... 65
HIS NAME WAS JESUS ... 66
THE POWER AND MAJESTY OF THE ELEMENTS ... 68

### CHAPTER III  LIFE CHANGING ... 75

TRANSFIGURATION—A CHANGE THAT GLORIFIES
   OR EXALTS ... 75
MOSES COMES FIRST ... 76
THE STORY OF JONAH'S NEAR DEATH EXPERIENCE ... 79
IT IS A "SOUL" JOURNEY ... 82

## PART III  TREASURES IN THE KINGDOM OF HEAVEN ... 85

### CHAPTER I  KNOWING ELIJAH ... 87

| | |
|---|---|
| HAPPY BIRTHDAY ELIJAH | 88 |
| THE MASS AWAKENING—A SPIRITUAL TRANSFORMATION | 90 |
| THE CHRIST CONSCIOUSNESS | 91 |

**CHAPTER II     BETTER THAN THE TIME BEFORE     92**

| | |
|---|---|
| THE AGE OF AQUARIUS—THE GOLDEN AGE | 92 |
| THE EARTH REINCARNATED | 93 |
| EVOLUTION | 94 |

**CHAPTER III     MOTHER, FATHER, GOD     95**

| | |
|---|---|
| THE TWINS | 95 |
| JACOB'S HOMECOMING | 96 |
| ISRAEL | 97 |
| JACOB | 97 |
| JACOB AND ESAU'S BIRTH | 98 |

**CHAPTER IV     SIGNS OF THE TIMES     103**

| | |
|---|---|
| STAIRWAY TO HEAVEN | 103 |
| JACOB'S INNER STRUGGLE | 107 |
| THE COAT OF MANY COLOURS | 109 |
| JOSEPH THE DREAMER | 109 |
| COMING TO TERMS | 110 |
| GREAT TRIBULATION | 112 |
| JACOB IN THE OLD KINGDOM | 113 |
| JACOB'S BLESSING | 115 |

**CHAPTER V     CHANGING OF THE GUARDS     116**

| | |
|---|---|
| AWARENESS | 116 |
| ACCEPTANCE | 116 |
| TRANSITION | 117 |

**CHAPTER VI     SEALED WITH A KISS     118**

| | |
|---|---|
| A SOUL PURPOSE | 119 |
| THE TWELVE (12) SONS/TRIBES OF JACOB/ISRAEL | 120 |
| BRING JACOB HOME AGAIN | 123 |
| FIG TREE LEAF TAKEN FROM NIMROD | 124 |
| THE TWO TRIBES IN THE SOUTH ARE NOT HIDDEN | 124 |

## PART IV  THE GREAT INVISIBLE SPIRIT — 127

### CHAPTER I     I AM, GREATER THAN EVER — 129

| | |
|---|---|
| ELIJAH | 130 |
| WIDOW OF ZAREPHATH | 132 |
| ELIJAH SAVES JONAH | 134 |
| WHY ARE YOU HERE? | 135 |
| TRADING PLACES | 136 |

### CHAPTER II     TRUTH — 139

| | |
|---|---|
| MOSES REINCARNATED | 139 |
| ELIJAH REINCARNATED | 145 |
| TRANSFIGURATION | 145 |
| WHO IS APOSTLE PAUL? | 146 |

### CHAPTER III     THE WORLD TO COME—OUR KINGDOM COME — 150

| | |
|---|---|
| A SPIRITUAL POINT WHERE REALITY EMERGES | 150 |
| WHO ARE THE 144,000? | 152 |
| CLEARING THE HAY | 154 |
| THE TRIBES OF ISRAEL—SONS OF JACOB | 155 |

### CHAPTER IV     THE SOUL KNOWS — 158

| | |
|---|---|
| YOUR SOUL FAMILY | 158 |
| KARMA | 159 |
| WORKING OUT YOUR KARMA | 160 |
| SUFFERING BROUGHT HIM GREAT JOY | 160 |
| I COULD NOT SEE—I COULD NOT HEAR | 163 |

| | | |
|---|---|---|
| **CHAPTER V** | **THE NEW AGE—THE GOLDEN AGE** | 166 |

    ENERGETIC SIGNATURE—COAT OF MANY COLOURS   166
    GOD WILL INCREASE   169
    SPIRIT DREAMS   169
    JOSEPH THE LIGHT WORKER   171
    ANGELS AMONG US   175
    BROTHERS SENT TO THE OLD KINGDOM—EGYPT   177
    THE SILVER LINING   178

| | | |
|---|---|---|
| **CHAPTER VI** | **THE PROMISED LAND** | 181 |

    THE HOLY BOOK WITHIN JOSEPH   181
    JACOB'S REQUEST TO GO HOME TO THE PROMISED LAND   182
    DIVINE PROMISE   183
    JOSEPH'S REQUEST TO GO HOME TO THE PROMISED LAND   187
    JACOB'S LADDER—SONS OF JACOB TO RISE OR CLIMB OUT OF BONDAGE   187
    THE LAND OF THE CHRIST CONSCIOUSNESS   189

| | | |
|---|---|---|
| *PART V* | *THE HOLY BOOK* | 191 |

| | | |
|---|---|---|
| **CHAPTER I** | **EVERYTHING IS CONNECTED** | 193 |

    "I FEEL THEREFORE I AM" SANETHA   193
    THE CHAKRAS   194
    DNA BLUEPRINTS AND ELEMENTS   195
    IN MY FATHER'S HOUSE ARE MANY MANSIONS   197
    THE PINEAL GLAND   198
    THE THIRD EYE   199

| | | |
|---|---|---|
| **CHAPTER II** | **WEAVING THE PIECES** | 200 |

    "I THINK THEREFORE I AM"   200
    SLEEPING DNA   204
    OIL—OUR WILL   205

| | | |
|---|---|---|
| YOUR DIVINE BLUEPRINT | | 208 |
| MISSING LINK NOT MISSING | | 209 |

## PART VI  THE BEGINNING — 213

### CHAPTER I    AN OPEN BOOK ENCODED IN THE REALMS OF LIGHT — 215

| | |
|---|---|
| THE ENERGY OF LOVE | 215 |
| INVISIBLE TO VISIBLE: BEYOND THE VEIL | 216 |
| REINCARNATION | 218 |
| NEW BEGINNINGS | 219 |

### CHAPTER II    IT IS YOU WE HAVE BEEN WAITING FOR — 221

| | |
|---|---|
| THE GOLDEN AGE | 221 |
| THE FIG TREE | 225 |
| A REASON FOR EVERYTHING | 226 |

### CHAPTER III    UNSOLVED MYSTERIES OF THE UNIVERSE — 229

| | |
|---|---|
| THOUGHT IS ENERGY | 229 |
| HEAVEN ON EARTH | 230 |
| THE BEGINNING OF THE END IS NOW | 234 |
| IN THE BEGINNING GOD CREATED HEAVEN AND EARTH | 235 |
| AWAKEN THE SLEEPING GIANT WITHIN | 238 |

*This book is dedicated to our beloved son, Michael*☺

*September 8th, 1977-September 11th, 2011*

**Matthew 5:8** Blessed are the pure in heart: for they shall see God.

## *Acknowledgments*

*It is deep within my heart and my soul that I am so very grateful to our Creator, all of the Angels, Spirit Guides and Ascended Masters, **AND** all of my loving families, friends, acquaintances, spiritual teachers and YOU reading this, for your guidance and teachings throughout history so that all of us could find our way home again.*

*A special thanks to the love of this life (possibly the love of many of my lives), my dear husband Lonnie of 38 plus years for always "being" there, believing and trusting me, myself and I and of course whoever else might appear☺*

*To my mother, father, children, grandchildren and future great grandchildren—I see you, I hear you and I love you forever and ever no matter where your spirit resides☺*

*To my soul family who have played and/or playing out the most difficult and unpleasant roles assisting and teaching me and many others so that we can help the masses who will be seeking this information—I give you praise and heartfelt forgiveness with the grandest of gratitude—for if it wasn't for you the hardest lessons would have been missed. We will hold the door open for you—our job won't be done till "olive" us come home.*

*Thank you so much to Spirit Library http://spiritlibrary.com for being there holding a place for me and the thousands of other "lightworkers" who have been working the trenches for so very long. Receiving daily inspirations of hope, love, joy and enlightenment from so many spiritual teachers has been one of my greatest gifts. I hope others will also contribute to your site to show their appreciation for all that you have done for so many on both sides of the veil!*

*Thank you to Dr Eric Pearl of The Reconnection www.thereconnection.com for following your heart so that I would find you and in the process find me which of course will help thousands of others find their way home. I am in **awe** of this healing work and your guidance has truly been a major turning point in this life where I have walked through the door right on to the other side!*

# SYNOPSIS

THE KINGDOM of HEAVEN within THE HOLY BOOK of THE GREAT INVISIBLE SPIRIT☺

The spiritual subject of past lives and reincarnation is highly controversial. Most religions don't believe it and science cannot prove it yet.

This book is an "Energy Healing Communication" with a DNA surprise, assisting to integrate and understand the deep-seated truths about who we are and where we came from. The information explains what is happening to us, the earth and the universe, and what one needs to do to adapt to the new energies on the planet at this time and for the years to come.

Within these pages contain a profound message with the new energy—a message that I have delivered many times over my many lifetimes. Who AM I? and Where do I come from? are questions that have been on the minds of everyone since the beginning. These thoughts are imprinted in our basic DNA.

My message is time-sensitive—to be ready for the masses who will be searching for this information at this exact time in history—the mass shift in consciousness. I am a very old soul who has been chosen for this task and accepted the challenge throughout history.

When I became aware of whom I was in the previous lifetime just before this one (less than five months between lives)—my newfound identity propelled me into the search for the answers to the questions gnawing at my soul. Each answer provided new questions, leading me down the enlightened path to an encounter with the "Grand Divine Plan".

I had no previous experience writing in this life, although during my search, I acquired a vintage copy of a book I wrote in my previous life. Since then, I have found several writings from other lifetimes all aligning with my soul signature. We all have gifts and abilities unimaginable, ready for anyone who walks through the door.

My search brought me into an awareness of *knowing* many of my past lives. It also revealed that my purpose of discovering was not about whom I was, but that I would write about past lives and reincarnation at a time on the planet when this information would be so needed.

I am co-writing a follow-up book, to be available soon. I have also started to write a third book about my lives—my soul journey.

Love & Light, *Sanetha*

# PART I

# *Souly Truth*

**John 8:32** (KJV)
[32] And ye shall know the truth, and the truth shall make you free.

## *Introduction*

# THE TIME IS NOW!

***Romans 13:11***
*And that, knowing the time, that now it is high time to awake out of sleep: for now is our salvation nearer than when we believed.*

I've always known about past lives and believed in reincarnation. I've experienced many times feelings of having been here before. I had no real interest in anything past that *knowing* until the one day when I discovered my name in my previous life. I reincarnated less than five months after leaving that life into this one.

Reincarnation makes perfect sense and, as you read this book many unexplained mysteries will become aha revelations! Reincarnation and past lives bring an entire new set of variables, especially when there has been little or no experience of the widespread independence that suddenly surrounds the seeker. Freedom often means that the old logic, the old lifestyle, most of the knowledge and assumptions simply obvious before no longer work. A new set of variables, priorities, even values come into play whether you are ready for them or not. It is our human nature to recreate or reinvent whenever we are trying to make something work better and that's exactly what we do when we reincarnate into our next life.

**Romans 16:25 (KJV)**
[25]*Now to him that is of power to stablish you according to my gospel, and the preaching of Jesus Christ, according to the revelation of the mystery, which was kept secret since the world began,*

This is the shocking and controversial truth—most religions don't believe and science can't prove yet. It is time to read between the lines and time to see the world with a new set of eyes—no more secrets, not even from you!

**Daniel 12:1-4 (KJV)**
*[1]And at that time shall Michael stand up, the great prince which standeth for the children of thy people: and there shall be a time of trouble, such as never was since there was a nation even to that same time: and at that time thy people shall be delivered, every one that shall be found written in the book.*

*[2]And many of them that sleep in the dust of the Earth shall awake, some to everlasting life, and some to shame and everlasting contempt.*

*[3]And they that be wise shall shine as the brightness of the firmament; and they that turn many to righteousness as the stars for ever and ever.*

*[4]But thou, O Daniel, shut up the words, and seal the book, even to the time of the end: many shall run to and fro, and knowledge shall be increased.*

An awakening human race is ready to know the truth—although some truths we learn may be difficult, even painful, to acknowledge. Important beliefs we were initially taught since childhood are disintegrating, ending one by one.

**John 8:32 (KJV)**
*[32]And ye shall know the truth, and the truth shall make you free.*

Some people have built their entire lives around false beliefs: the ones learned from families they grew up with or the ones they learned from institutions like our school systems, military, governments, certain spiritual teachings and religions.

We learn to live by certain principles based upon those beliefs and we often hold on to them long after they are useful. The familiarity, sense of belonging and illusion of safety these beliefs offer provide a cherished comfort zone.

**1 Corinthians 2:7-16 (KJV)**
*[7] But we speak the wisdom of God in a mystery, even the hidden wisdom, which God ordained before the world unto our glory: [8] Which none of the princes of this world knew: for had they known it, they would not have crucified the Lord of glory.*

*[9] But as it is written, Eye hath not seen, nor ear heard, neither have entered into the heart of man, the things which God hath prepared for them that love him. [10] But God hath revealed them unto us by his Spirit: for the Spirit searcheth all things, yea, the deep things of God.*

*[11] For what man knoweth the things of a man, save the spirit of man which is in him? even so the things of God knoweth no man, but the Spirit of God. [12] Now we have received, not the spirit of the world, but the spirit which is of God; that we might know the things that are freely given to us of God. [13] Which things also we speak, not in the words which man's wisdom teacheth, but which the Holy Ghost teacheth; comparing spiritual things with spiritual.*

*[14] But the natural man receiveth not the things of the Spirit of God: for they are foolishness unto him: neither can he know them, because they are spiritually discerned. [15] But he that is spiritual judgeth all things, yet he himself is judged of no man. [16] For who hath known the mind of the Lord, that he may instruct him? but we have the mind of Christ.*

The Bible, as well as other religious and spiritual texts, have provided insights based on how the information was presented. We know that most of the writings have been altered time and time again—disintegrating the original message, changing the energy, leaving only hints of truth barely recognizable to the human eye.

The Bible quotes in this book have been taken from the King James Version—an older version of the Bible texts, yet this version is not the original biblical texts written so many lifetimes ago. It is my intent that the quotes that are only pieces of the truth be received only as a doorway to a bigger truth.

Many people do not like change; change takes you out of your comfort zone. Truth is not always welcome and is often met with great resistance, even hostility and hatred. In particular, beliefs affiliated with major world religions have been the underlying reasons that instigated and continue to instigate brutal wars, horrific genocide and murderous crusades that sadly even persist to this day in certain areas of the world.

Not all for nothing—there is a reason for everything. Good, Bad, Love and Hate—we need to experience pain and suffering and sorrow to know joy and love and happiness! We have evolved onto a "New Earth". The new energy, the frequencies that are available, offer "paradise on Earth" for those who seek their truth.

Since the days of Adam and Eve when they ate the fruit from the tree of life, all of us have lived lifetimes hidden behind a veil—not knowing who we are or where we came from. We are with the understanding of our own burdens deep within our consciousness, the identification of the heavy baggage that blocks our spiritual identity.

We are risking reaching out for that freedom, taking responsibility of free will, risking crossing unknown boundaries and breaking down walls, walking down the back roads and the discomfort that can come from new beginnings and venturing into the world with a deep belief in the promise of a better world.

Do you have the willingness to *hear* new things and invite new wisdom to prepare the way to the Kingdom of Heaven within the Holy Book of The Great Invisible Spirit☺? As long as we fail to acknowledge our *vision* of reality, our truth will remain incomplete. Spiritual growth is the process of venturing beyond one's boundaries into unfamiliar territory where the deeper truth can only be known out of an encounter with the unknown. There are no mistakes.

We are all individuals coming to the table with various stories, baggage, and different agendas. If we remain open and allow in our minds and hearts for the stranger that would deepen our understanding and broaden our sight, we will celebrate in unity with our Creator God and All That Is till "all of us" find our way home.

It is my purpose and has been my soul purpose since the beginning, as I was appointed to *"bring the knowledge of and the ability to have paradise or Heaven on Earth."* We all have a divine purpose and a divine plan—one with our Creator. We are here together at this exact point in time to help each other learn, understand, unravel the mysteries of life, and discover our spiritual selves. There is a reason why it is now.

## Chapter 1

# THE TRUTH WILL SET YOU FREE

### *Adam & Eve, Not the First on Earth*

**Genesis 3 (KJV)**
[20]*And Adam called his wife's name Eve; because she was the mother of all living.*

One could interpret the story of Adam and Eve, the first man and woman as being the first to know good from evil, eating from the tree of knowledge between good and evil being a symbol of this.

**Colossians 1:15-17 (KJV)**
[15]*Who is the image of the invisible God, the firstborn of every creature:* [16]*For by him were all things created, that are in heaven, and that are in Earth, visible and invisible, whether they be thrones, or dominions, or principalities, or powers: all things were created by him, and for him:* [17]*And he is before all things, and by him all things consist.*

**Genesis 3 (KJV)**
[3]*But of the fruit of the tree which is in the midst of the garden, God hath said, Ye shall not eat of it, neither shall ye touch it, lest ye die.*

If you eat the fruit of the tree, if you sin, you will die but not a physical death. This is a spiritual death in the sense that we would become disconnected from our spiritual beings and in a sense the spirits have been sleeping; "die" means sleep. When Adam and Eve ate the fruit, this was the beginning of our disconnection from our Creator and from ourselves forgetting our knowledge, gifts and abilities.

We haven't been able to remember who we are, where we came from or even why we are here—a divine plan created for our spiritual and physical evolution.

The knowledge of and the ability to have Paradise or Heaven on Earth has been well preserved over the eons of time. Before Adam died, he passed the knowledge of and the ability to his son, Seth.

While some may think that evolution doesn't require a supreme being, it doesn't rule out the existence or involvement of such a being either. Much of the anxiety about evolution stems from the fear that in accepting the theory, one denies the existence of God.

The same anxiety and fear revolve around the subjects of past lives and reincarnation. Many are searching for knowledge, information and answers to questions about themselves and the higher powers of the Universe.

Scientists acknowledge that there are some questions science simply cannot answer. We do not know who the first person to live was; it was long before the time attributed to Adam and Eve. Humans have evolved over millions of years. There is ample evidence of this process and skeletal remains of a large number of primitive individuals have been found and dated scientifically.

A spiritual transition is underway. This information will spawn new thoughts and new ideas, bringing the spiritual and scientific worlds together. The world is not ending on December 21, 2012, or anytime after that; the world will not exist as you know it—it has evolved into a greater and better world.

## SETH

His name meaning "placed or appointed", Seth was the third son of Adam and Eve and brother of Cain and Able. According to Genesis 4:25, Seth was born after the slaying of Abel by Cain, and Eve believed God had appointed him as a replacement for Abel.

*Genesis 4:25 (KJV)*
*²⁵And Adam knew his wife again; and she bare a son, and called his name Seth: For God, said she, hath appointed me another seed instead of Abel, whom Cain slew.*

In the Antiquities of the Jews, Josephus refers to Seth as virtuous and of excellent character, and reports that his descendants invented the wisdom of the heavenly bodies and built the "pillars of the sons of Seth", two pillars inscribed with many scientific discoveries and inventions, notably in astronomy. They were built by Seth's descendants based on Adam's prediction that the world would be destroyed at one time by fire and another time by global flood, in order to protect the discoveries and be remembered after the destruction. One was composed of brick and the other of stone, so that if the pillar of brick should be destroyed, the pillar of stone would remain, both reporting the ancient discoveries and informing men that a pillar of brick was also erected. Josephus reports that the pillar of stone remained in the land of Siriad in his day.

*Seth married his "soul sister" Azura*

The Bible mentions sons marrying their sisters. Are you aware of "soul family" or perhaps you have forgotten? According to Jewish tradition, Azura is the twin sister of the biblical Abel and becomes the wife of Seth.

The interpretation of words and other communications during history has devolved; order has devolved into anarchy. It is more than probable that Seth married his twin flame and not his brother's twin sister.

Soul families are souls we have met and lived with in many lifetimes. They have been our lovers, spouses, mothers, fathers, sisters, brothers, teachers, students, friends, family and, yes, enemies.

Twin souls, also called Twin Flames or Twin Rays, are the other half of your soul. We are all parts of the Divine Being, God, All That Is, Source, Spirit and The Creator. The final splitting of the many neutrally gendered souls created male and female halves of a whole, the Twin Soul.

As spiritual beings, we have lived many lives with several of our "soul family". Sometimes they are husbands or wives, sons or daughters, grandparents, uncles or aunts, cousins or friends, or acquaintances or even our enemies, victims or tormenters. We contract with these souls to return to Earth together for greater learning and growth. We must experience both male and female roles—a balance of yin and yang.

The deepest soul relationships, especially those we call a soul brother, a soul sister or a soul mate, call upon us to face our deepest fears, release our deepest wounds, and take an awesome leap of courage into the unknown.

We are here in this third-dimensional world, but we are also present in other, higher-dimensional realities simultaneously with our soul family. For example, like me, some of you also came from the Sirius star system, which is sixth dimensional.

We have soul family on these other worlds, and they have been our family for longer than we have been reincarnating on Earth. We originate from a source where we are nurtured until it is time to go out into the unknown. This reminds me of sending our children off to kindergarten or when they leave the nest.

Who am I? Where did I come from? These questions are the basic tools given to each soul who incarnates into the physical form, imprinted in our DNA. Asking these questions throughout our lifetimes has paved the road leading us down the path to getting us home.

Just when we think we have it all figured out, we are presented with new sets of mind-boggling details that lead us down yet another path. Life and other things have gotten in your way and now something has sparked your attention and you are ready for more.

## WHO AM I?

I AM SANETHA, the third daughter of Eve. My soul purpose is to *bring the knowledge of and ability to live in Heaven or Paradise on Earth.*

The name "Sanetha" was given to me from spirit during the creation of this book. Sanetha is a meld of my name in this life (Annetta Renee) and my names in other lives.

I am a spiritual being having another glorious human experience☺. I am a lightworker and world server. I am a spiritual, clairsentient healer and interpreter. It is my **destiny** to bring this information to the planet at this time in history, which has been sealed from blind eyes and deaf ears. As humanity starts to awaken, this message will be there for anyone who is ready just at the right time—NOW!

I continue to bring the same message that I have delivered in many lifetimes before. With each incarnation, like me, my message has returned stronger and better than the time before. During this time in history, the message comes with a new energy—a higher frequency matching the vibration of the New Earth in a way that will change many lives past, present and future.

I have written on these matters several times before to help you discover your own spiritual truth so that we together can bring Jacob back home again.

There are many others who have also come here to deliver messages of great importance at this time on Earth through books, movies and other forms of communication that will help the masses who are ready to awaken. Are you one of them?

**"I hope that posterity will judge me kindly, not only as to the things which I have explained, but also to those which I have intentionally omitted so as to leave to others the pleasure of discovery."—Rene Descartes**

I have had 271 lives on planet Earth, and more than 3,400 lives in total on other planets and star systems. After creation from "Source", my first life form was on the star Sirius.

The **Sirians** are more advanced in the metaphysical sense as Sirius is one of the more advanced training centers or universities to which the ascended masters travel. Sirius has a direct link with our solar system and the Sirians have been amongst us since the time of the Mayan and Egyptian civilizations.

They gave the Egyptians much advanced astronomical and medical information and also gave the Mayan race advanced knowledge. They helped the Earth during the time of the cataclysmic period in Atlantis. Sirius is a star system that is a meeting place for Earth beings who wish to continue their spiritual studies. The Sirians helped to build the Pyramids and temples of Egypt and they are involved with helping Earth into this new Golden Age.

**According to Wikipedia, Sirius** is the brightest star in the night sky. The name "Sirius" is derived from the ancient Greek: Σείριος *Seirios* ("glowing" or "scorcher"). Sirius is also known colloquially as the **"Dog Star"**, reflecting its prominence in its constellation, Canis Major (Greater Dog). The heliacal rising of Sirius marked the flooding of the Nile in ancient Egypt and the "dog days" of summer for the ancient Greeks, while to the Polynesians it marked winter and was an important star for navigation around the Pacific Ocean.

Like many of you, I have existed on both lost continents Lemuria and Atlantis. Mainstream history has chosen to forget about the lost continent of Lemuria that once existed in the Pacific. Lemuria was an ancient civilization that existed prior to and during the time of Atlantis. Physically, Lemuria existed largely in the Southern Pacific, between North America and Asia/Australia. Lemuria is also sometimes referred to as Mu, or the Motherland (of Mu). At the peak of their civilization, the Lemurian people were both highly evolved and very spiritual. While concrete physical evidence of this ancient continent may be difficult to find, many people "know" that they have a strong connection to Lemuria.

## *We are ONE*

In this life, my parents had five daughters; I AM the middle seed☺. My being in the middle gave me a greater opportunity to stay connected and communicate with my angels and guides. There is a reason for everything.

I also have a brother who has a different mother. I now understand the significance behind the experience that had to be. There are no mistakes.

I married my high school sweetheart, a first-born son who also has three older sisters and two younger brothers—one brother has a different mother and the other brother has a different mother and a different father. His vision is unique—an advantage of knowing how to proceed, an insight to viewing what is coming and *seeing* the end result.

Our first-born son has twins—a boy and a girl. Our first-born daughter has a son and our second-born son has no children.

**John 1:29 (KJV)**
*²⁹The next day John seeth Jesus coming unto him, and saith, Behold the Lamb of God, which taketh away the sin of the world.*

I took up a number of different careers along the way. I had almost as many careers it seems as I have had lifetimes. I worked hard at everything—there are no mistakes. There is a purpose in each of my endeavors, as there is in yours.

The universe always worked it out that we had just enough. Whenever it seemed we didn't have money for life's necessities, the money would somehow appear. I often prayed to God with my guides and angels by my side, asking them to help us through the rough times. Just like many of you, I had a lot of worry and fear that life brings. Our three children are our true pride and our glory. We did whatever it took to be a happy, healthy family. Life has its twists and turns, some that really hurt. There is a reason for everything; there are no mistakes.

While writing this book, my oldest son made another journey back home to our Creator on the other side. He is my guide, a guiding light assisting many of the masses who are ascending into the new frequencies at this time on the "New Earth". It was his plan, our plan, your plan, too. He is a God-spark with a divine purpose, a spirit who guides me; his light is bright, his love unconditional!

*"The law of Love could be best understood and learned through little children."*—Mahatma Gandhi (1869-1948)

When my grandson was only 10 years old, we experienced the loss of his great grandmother, my mother. He was feeling the loss and could see how it was affecting the rest of us. He wanted to help himself and all of us come to terms with our sorrow we were feeling. He wrote:

*"Heaven's shore just above with all the family that loves. It's the world that's not ending its life—let it rest with no pain in a peaceful place Heaven."*—**Gavin Goetz**

I am a strong, spiritual being, yet my heart aches to the depths of my soul. There is no pain or sorrow greater than I know. They are part of us; you never expect that they will ever go to be the spirit on the other side where we cannot *see* them with these old eyes.

Losing loved ones, including our pets who are so very dear, is truly the hardest sorrow to endure. I walk with him in the thin air; I can feel his hand is near. Every day is but clearer to when I will *see* him in the mirror.

No wonder I have loved the movie Lady Hawk so much over the years! The man turns into a wolf by night and the lady into a hawk by day; they get a glimpse of each other for a brief second as the sun comes up in the early dawn and then as the sun goes down in the early dusk.

We are all so very blessed with the presence of their loving spirits—a soul never dies, we must let them fly. They are "Great Invisible Spirits" who are always with you forever and ever. The time has come for you to *see* with a new set of eyes, *hear* with a new set of ears so that you can *feel* "all that is". ☺

It's your view of change that makes the biggest difference in your life. *"If you keep doing what you've always done, you'll keep getting what you've always gotten."*—Jim Rohn

*"Be the change you wish to see in the world."*—Mahatma Gandhi (1869-1948)

## LOVE Conquers ALL—THE DOORS OPEN

The door stood wide open and the Universe was definitely calling. But what exactly was it saying? There really is only one way to find out—walk right on through the door to see what is waiting on the other side. ☺

It was a constant struggle and pulling of my heart strings and very uncomfortable being in unfamiliar territory. When I came to Connecticut to be with my husband, my heart pulled and yearned for my children home in Canada. When I came back to Canada to be with my children, my heart pulled and yearned again, but now for my husband. It was confusing and it took every cell in my body to work it out until the uncomfortable became more comfortable. It took years to smooth out the irregular heartbeat! There is a reason for everything.

I was never one for staying home, watching soaps, or getting into any particular kind of hobby like sewing, knitting, gourmet cooking or tropical planting. I guess you could say I got by and kept a tidy house and happy family, but I wasn't a Martha Stewart by any means. It wasn't in my personality. I was always looking for that something else, not knowing what that really was. I was digging—a seeker of knowledge and information.

When hurricane Katrina hit the state of Louisiana, I felt so unworthy, hopeless and useless. The same overwhelming, deep feelings came over me the day of September 11—only this time I had spare time on my hands and I felt I should be doing something—something really BIG!

I was praying for all of the people who were suffering and praying that I could be of some help for someone over there. I was a volunteer for the Red Cross in Connecticut, but I knew I could do more. I was so frustrated with the situation. I began to demand answers from spirit to the constant questions that nattered in my head.

*"What exactly do you have in mind for me? It must be something really BIG because why else would you be so set on my having so much free time on my hands—and having everything one could want except all my family near me? And why would you be so set on me being alone so many hours in the day, when so much help is needed everywhere you look?"*

There are no mistakes and think again if you believe in a coincidence. Everything happens for a reason. Every single detail—including your name, your family, your career choices—even the fact that you are reading this book is not a coincidence. ☺

Divine Guidance and Divine Timing are always at play. Some of you know exactly what I am talking about, and others may not understand right now. More than likely you have sent a thought out to the Universe that brought you here reading this book—something caught your eye or your ears. You may have had thoughts or ideas twirling around in your head and now you are reading this book. It was part of the plan you made very long ago. It has always been in the plan you made; our spirit guides made the plan with you to help each other find our way.

They have their ways and you will soon see how this plan has been moving forward unbeknownst to you!

*"All the world's a stage, and all the men and women merely players: they have their exits and their entrances; and one man in his time plays many parts, his acts being seven ages."*—William Shakespeare

When you were born, in most cases your family brought you up into their way of living in this life that they knew best. There is a reason for everything. You developed beliefs based on the information that was given to you. Some of you may have thoughts or ideas about other possibilities from time to time. With every question, there is always an answer.

Have you ever experienced one of those moments when you were looking for something but you couldn't quite put your finger on it? Or how about when you had something on your mind—you were trying to tell someone about it—it was on the tip of your tongue and you couldn't quite get it to come out!

You are going out the door, and you know you forgot something but you cannot for the **life** of you remember or imagine what it is? Oh then there is the odd time now and then when you feel like you've been there before—in fact, the entire place, people and words all feel so familiar.

Have you noticed that the same uncomfortable situations arise in your life over and over again? Have you confronted them? Do you walk around them? Or even worse, turn around and go the other way?

Many of us have had these experiences leaving us perplexed and bewildered! Take a moment or two and try to remember what exactly it is that you have forgotten.

Is fear, worry and doubt keeping you from moving forward? Are you ready for a truth you have awaited for so long? Not everyone is willing to walk through that door. If you are willing to open up to other possibilities and probabilities, the Holy Book within is yours to discover through the Great Invisible Spirit. ☺

*"Each problem that I solved became a rule, which served afterwards to solve other problems."*—Rene Descartes

## The Search for the Holy Grail

Absolutely everyone has been searching for the "Holy Grail" high and low, to and fro! Surprise—it is right under your nose. ☺

**Daniel 12:4 (KJV)**
⁴*But thou, O Daniel, shut up the words, and seal the book, even to the time of the end: many shall run to and fro, and knowledge shall be increased.*

The "Holy Grail" plays a different role everywhere it appears, but in most versions of the legend the hero must prove himself worthy to be in its presence. In the early tales, Percival's immaturity prevents him from fulfilling his destiny when he first encounters the Grail, and he must grow spiritually and mentally before he can locate it again. Later, information reveals the Grail is a symbol of God's grace, available to all but only fully realized by those who prepare themselves spiritually, like the saintly Galahad. He is the illegitimate son of Lancelot and Elaine of Corbenic, and is renowned for his gallantry and purity.

The "Grail" (in medieval legend) is the cup or platter used by Jesus at the Last Supper, and in which Joseph of Arimathea received Christ's blood. The Holy Grail is highly pursued and sought after.

## The Great Invisible Spirit

I was walking along my path one day when I came upon a mysterious object. A glimmer of light coming from the heavenly, sunshiny summer sky happened to beam a beautiful, brilliant spark just as I was coming around the bend.

At first glance, it seemed like just another rock that I wanted to ignore. I asked myself, why does that ol' rock keep showing up at my door? So instead of walking around it or turning completely around, I decided to take a closer look. Was it a stone, a fossil, a lost gem, secrets to the Universe? Whatever it was, I wanted to KNOW. I stopped and recognized that I had seen this somewhere many times before.

I had a feeling perhaps there was something more, so I picked it up and put it in my pocket. A few steps down the path, I found a shady tree beside a gentle stream of water. I sat down on the ground under the tree and took the mystery piece out of my pocket so that I could learn more. I held it in my hand close to my heart and asked, *"What do you want from me?"*

What could this possibly be? THEN, when I really began to *see,* a *feeling* came over me. This was very interesting and I started to look for more. The more I *saw,* the more I could *hear.* The more I could *hear,* the *feeling* was very clear.

The surprises, the mysteries, the gifts and the abilities are all there just waiting for you if you seek. Sometimes I put them in my pocket for a minute and other times for a day or two. However, there are times that I may need to keep these little gems for weeks, months, years—and YES, I have kept them for many lifetimes!

My path has become an open field with mountains so tall and oceans so deep and blue. My journey has taken me to the heart and soul of "ALL THAT IS".

### *"The Kingdom of Heaven within The Holy Book of The Great Invisible Spirit*☺

> "Again, the kingdom of heaven is like unto treasure hid in a field; the which when a man hath found, he hideth, and for joy thereof goeth and selleth all that he hath, and buyeth that field."
> **Matthew 13:44**

# Chapter 11

# THE GREAT BROTHERHOOD OF LIGHT

## *A COSMIC CYCLE*

Every 25,920 years or so, the Earth enters into the final stage of a cosmic cycle from the Piscean to the Aquarian Age, and son of man is faced with a choice. In the past, the Lemurian and Atlantean civilizations destroyed themselves with the knowledge of technology they had gained. It will be different this time—The Kingdom of Heaven within the Holy Book of the Great Invisible Spirit ☺ is not accessible to those who do not have the mark of the beast.

**Revelation 13:16-18(KJV)**
*[16]And he causeth all, both small and great, rich and poor, free and bond, to receive a mark in their right hand, or in their foreheads: [17]And that no man might buy or sell, save he that had the mark, or the name of the beast, or the number of his name. [18]Here is wisdom. Let him that hath understanding count the number of the beast: for it is the number of a man; and his number is Six hundred threescore and six.*

Help is being poured onto the Earth plane as the Earth goes into accelerated evolution. To help guide humanity through this final phase in the battle between good and evil, the Great Brotherhood of Light has been approaching ever closer the Earth plane, providing it with adepts and initiates who are their disciples, all working together under a grand divine plan. As these high beings mix with the Earthly populations, less and less shall there be the apparent distance between the spiritual and physical planes as the veils are removed.

All parts of our lives and the world will be influenced by the Great Brotherhood of Light as they draw near to son of man as this is all part of the divine plan to bring about the New Age, so long promised eons ago.

## SOME ROSES STINK and SOME SKUNKS SMELL PRETTY

Please STOP! Take time to smell the roses, even if they stink! ☐ There is always something there for you to take with you on your journey; take the bad with the good—everything happens for a reason. You must experience sadness to know joy. You must experience hate to know love.

***You will start to realize much more about yourself, your present lifetime experiences, and why you needed to have them☺—good or bad.***

Sometimes something uncomfortable comes along your path, but you tend to walk around it or turn around. You're thinking, "No way, not for me." You aren't even sure why you're thinking it isn't for you. You just sense a strong feeling of not wanting to go down that road. No worries, though, because it will come back to you again and again and again until you STOP right smack in front of it. Go ahead—walk through that door!

Instead of walking around it or turning around to avoid it completely, you are now acknowledging the mystery treasure on your path. The mystery treasures can come in any kind of energy form, such as objects, people, places, words, numbers by sight or by feeling. It very likely is a message that the Universe, your guides and your angels are trying to give you. The message is, *"**You need to take a look at this—there is something here for you that has much value that will help you to move forward on your path.**"* Life is a mystery—think of it as receiving clues that will solve the puzzle and discover the **"truths"** to the many unsolved mysteries.

Maybe you have reoccurring situations—for example, getting into the same bad relationships with different people over and over again, or problems with your career, money, family and addictions. Whatever it is, there is a reason why the same thing keeps coming back to you. Could there be a lesson to learn here somewhere? It is very probable that the Universe has been trying to get in touch with you, but you are ignoring everything! Deaf ears perhaps—or maybe you are blind?

## *PAY ATTENTION! Time to wake up!*

*"But as it is written, Eye hath not seen, nor ear heard, neither have entered into the heart of man, the things which God hath prepared for them that love him.*

### 1 *Coriathians 2:9 (KJV)*
*"Wherefore he saith, Awake thou that sleepest, and arise from the dead, and Christ shall give thee light."—**Ephesians 5:14 (KJV)***

### *The Road Less Travelled—The Path Widens*

Along the way, I saw another path. I was very comfortable on this one and I didn't want to veer too far off the "ol' beaten path". I knew I was safe there because I could see many other souls walking the same road day after day. Then one day, I decided I needed a new route. This ol' path was getting boring and I needed fresh, new ideas. If I was going to make a difference in the world, I knew I would need to be bold and brave, too. It was like entering into a field of dreams—the pickings are abundant and ripe! My cup runneth over . . .

Genesis 49:22-25 (KJV)
[22] *Joseph is a fruitful bough, even a fruitful bough by a well; whose branches run over the wall:*[23] *The archers have sorely grieved him, and shot at him, and hated him:*[24] *But his bow abode in strength, and the*

*arms of his hands were made strong by the hands of the mighty God of Jacob; (from thence is the shepherd, the stone of Israel:)*

I picked up a very mysterious information packet which led me to **know** not only my life purposes, but also my soul purpose, too. I discovered who I was in my previous life, including my name in that life, career, family and other details. I knew it was a very rare find and even more rare that I learned I had reincarnated into this physical body in such a short time—less than five months after leaving that life.

I have always believed in reincarnation, yet this was *"shock and awe"* in every sense of the words on an entirely new level most of us have never, ever experienced—and then *"the plot thickens."* I became aware of several of my past lives. This was the tip of the kingdom of what I was about to unveil. ☺

How do I KNOW? WHY do I KNOW? These were the two BIG questions that immediately popped into my pineal gland that particular day. Who wanted me to know? What should I do with this KNOWING? Should I be contacting someone? One question rolled into another question. Should I tell my husband that I was a male orthopedic surgeon who died the same year that I was born into this life? ☺ My mother who passed away a few months before this had spent her life in and out of orthopedic surgeon offices!

I found an astonishing amount of details of that life including a biography and a book I cowrote in that life. I purchased a vintage copy I found on e-bay. I couldn't get it out of my head. I was cautious because I didn't want this knowledge of my reincarnation to get out to my past life family members that most likely were still living in this life.

Over the next 18 to 20 months, my quest became the passions of my soul. As I progressed through my enlightened pathway, I was gently awakened to **"The Great Invisible Spirit within"**.

This book is written for humanity at this exact time in history to assist the masses of *people who are and who will be* searching for answers about their own spirituality. This book offers answers to the daunting questions that have forever been on the minds of everyone throughout the centuries, throughout history! It is information hidden but never lost, information so valuable it can change your life.

Each time I return into physical existence, I have returned to experience life under different circumstances and different roles. I am here to learn from others and I am also here to guide other souls who have made the journey with me. It is a soul group effort—with each individual soul playing a role—and the goal is to **"Bring Jacob Home"**. When we help others, we help ourselves. When we help ourselves, we help others.

## MULTIPLE LIFETIMES

Each lifetime, you have come to learn something new—a list of life purposes. The experiences are chalked up to a list of accomplishments with a goal to grow spiritually individually and in unity. If you don't accomplish something on the list, then next time you reincarnate you might try that again, only with a new set of circumstances, possibilities and probabilities all planned out with members of your soul family before you incarnate again.

It is from this list that your soul family, including your guides, angels and ascended masters, are working with you to help you accomplish the experiences you came here to learn. They too are part of the plan. Indeed, it is a tricky task to comprehend for the majority of us—that we are born knowing—and that then the programming begins and our memories start to fade.

## THERE ARE NO MISTAKES

Your family, friends, religion and other variables are all part of the plan. More amazing is that your guides, angels, ascended masters and your higher self are also very much interested in helping you succeed. If you succeed, then they too succeed. Your spiritual growth becomes their spiritual growth as well.

Circumstances, both good and bad, are set up as an attempt for you to remember what you came here to do. THERE IS NO RIGHT WAY; THERE IS NO WRONG WAY. Your sex, the color of your skin, where you were born, your name, your birthday are all important details. Everything, to the last dotted "eye" ☺, has been planned out with other souls who become your parents, your siblings, your children, your friends or just brief acquaintances.

Each of my lifetimes I have come to learn specific lessons through physical life experiences and events. The learning of these lessons may also be understood as your "life purpose(s)". One of the most important life lessons/purposes I carefully planned out prior to my incarnation into this lifetime is to learn **"interdependence"**.

From Wikipedia, the free encyclopedia:

**Interdependence** is a dynamic of being mutually and physically responsible to, and sharing a common set of principles with others. This concept differs distinctly from "dependence" in that an interdependent relationship implies that all participants are emotionally, economically, ecologically and or morally "interdependent." Some people advocate freedom or independence as a sort of ultimate good; others do the same with devotion to one's family, community, or society. Interdependence recognizes the truth in each position and weaves them together.

Two states that cooperate with each other are said to be interdependent. It can also be defined as the interconnectedness and the reliance on one another socially, economically, environmentally and politically.

Genesis 25:23 (KJV)
*[23] And the Lord said unto her, Two nations are in thy womb, and two manner of people shall be separated from thy bowels; and the one people shall be stronger than the other people; and the elder shall serve the younger.*

## Chapter III

# AS ABOVE, SO BELOW

*"As Above, So Below."*—**Hermes Trismegistos**

### *Finding Your Soul Purpose*

Do you feel you are on Earth to do something special but do not know what?

Are you yearning for a more meaningful life?

Do you realize you created a plan for your life before you were born?

Do you realize something within you **knows** all about this plan?

Do you know this is your soul?

Do you know that your soul will guide you step by step as your life plan/soul purpose unfolds?

Are you ready to claim your true identity?

Are you ready to access the gifts and abilities you have within?

Are you willing to do the work?

## THE SHIFT—3D to 5D

We are spiritual beings having a human experience. Most of us have heard that one over and over again. For some of you, it was enough to have you searching for more, while for others it would take a little more. There is a reason for everything. Each of us has a job to do—a LIFE purpose as well as a SOUL purpose. You agreed to be here and you planned the entire existence with a multitude of souls. Most of you do not remember this right now although you do have moments of ***déjà vu.*** ☺

When you are born, your soul enters the physical body sometime between conception and birth. As soon as you enter this plane of existence, for most of us there is a type of veil that conceals who we really are. This is because our physical body exists on the planet Earth that was located in the lowest dimension in the Universe—the third dimension. In actuality, the planet is in the process of moving into a higher dimension—the fifth dimension. An unveiling is underway—a rebirth—the Earth is reincarnating.

## NO FEAR—FEAR Feeds More Fear

***The world is ending as we know it on December 21, 2012.*** For most reading this book, that date has come and gone so many of you are relieved, yet you know something is very different. It is a change that can be referred to as "THE SHIFT". The shift in consciousness—a mass shift in consciousness—was predicted eons ago to occur at this time on Earth.

The magic date—December 21, 2012—is and was on the minds of almost everyone. It is pretty hard not to think about this date since it has become an icon in the marketplace. What is above is also below— the Cosmos, Universe, Earth and mankind are all in the process of shifting consciousness.

Be aware of your thoughts and emotions; if you are fearful or worried, that will mirror back to you in that form. The world won't look much different when you wake up on December 22$^{nd}$, 2012, unless we have a snowstorm or perhaps record-high temperatures just in time for Christmas. Many changes have been occurring gradually and will continue to change over the next few years that will change the world as we know it.

1987 was a momentous year that marked the beginning of humanity's ascension, rebirth and shift into the Fourth Dimension. 1987's Harmonic Convergence also marked the beginning of our sun's direct alignment with the center of our Milky Way Galaxy. This very rare cosmic event has been exposing our whole solar system to intense rounds of wave energy.

The newly discovered energy source emanating from Galactic Center is making it possible for the dormant part of our DNA to be awakened and setting in motion The Great Shift long prophesied by many indigenous traditions, including the Mayan, Incan, Hopi and Vedic. Mayan timekeepers records indicate that 2012 marks the close of several large cycles of time—a 26,000 year Mayan Calendar cycle—a 78,000 year Earth cycle—a 26 million year Evolution cycle—and the 225 million Galactic Year. The simultaneous close of these cycles in 2012 is like the odometer turning over for the entire history of our galaxy, and perhaps the whole Cosmos. It is a moment when humanity, Planet Earth, the Milky Way Galaxy and perhaps all of creation is expected to take a simultaneous leap in evolution. www.weinholds.org

The signs in the heavens point to an extraordinary renewal in the years just ahead. This happens every 2,000 years, the last one coinciding with the arrival of Christ. The powerful change that will sweep through the Cosmos, the shift in mood, action and intention, is evident. http://www.bibliotecapleyades.net/esp_2012_02.htm

## *The Time of the End—Not the End of Time*

It is the end of old beliefs and old systems. It is a time of extreme change. It is the end of an old cycle and the beginning of a new one—one of joy, happiness, love and light. ☺

In this period of accelerated evolution, all that has worked against our best interests will tumble, even the most sacred of religious, banking and political institutions. We are going through a vast worldwide weeding out process, removing the weeds out of the wheat field, "clearing the hay".

### Micah 3:11-12 (KJV)
*¹¹The heads thereof judge for reward, and the priests thereof teach for hire, and the prophets thereof divine for money: yet will they lean upon the LORD, and say, Is not the LORD among us? none evil can come upon us. ¹²Therefore shall Zion for your sake be plowed as a field, and Jerusalem shall become heaps, and the mountain of the house as the high places of the forest.*

Those dark souls that bring about negativity and conflict on Earth will be eventually moved off the Earth plane and the remaining good souls will be then allowed to proceed with their evolution. The seeds with "oil" will grow.

### Malachi 4
*__1__For, behold, the day cometh, that shall burn as an oven; and all the proud, yea, and all that do wickedly, shall be stubble: and the day that cometh shall burn them up, saith the LORD of hosts, that it shall leave them neither root nor branch. __2__But unto you that fear my name shall the Sun of righteousness arise with healing in his wings; and ye shall go forth, and grow up as calves of the stall. __3__And ye shall tread down the wicked; for they shall be ashes under the soles of your feet in the day that I shall do this, saith the LORD of hosts. __4__Remember ye **the law of Moses** my servant, which I commanded unto him in Horeb for all Israel, with the statutes and judgments. __5__Behold, I will send you **Elijah** the prophet before the coming of the great and dreadful day of the LORD: __6__And he shall turn the heart of the fathers to the children, and the heart of the children to their fathers, lest I come and smite the earth with a curse.*

## The Time of the End

Just as the words imply, what would you like to end in your life? Ask yourself what it is that no longer serves you in this life? What would you like to change that will make your life happier and healthier? Are you ready to end the pain and sorrow? Are you ready to end the separation from your God-given birthrights?

### Daniel 12 (KJV)
[1] And at that time shall Michael stand up, the great prince which standeth for the children of thy people: and there shall be a time of trouble, such as never was since there was a nation even to that same time: and at that time thy people shall be delivered, every one that shall be found written in the book. [2] And many of them that sleep in the dust of the earth shall awake, some to everlasting life, and some to shame and everlasting contempt. [3] And they that be wise shall shine as the brightness of the firmament; and they that turn many to righteousness as the stars for ever and ever. [4] But thou, O Daniel, shut up the words, and seal the book, even to the time of the end: many shall run to and fro, and knowledge shall be increased. [5] Then I Daniel looked, and, behold, there stood other two, the one on this side of the bank of the river, and the other on that side of the bank of the river. [6] And one said to the man clothed in linen, which was upon the waters of the river, How long shall it be to the end of these wonders? [7] And I heard the man clothed in linen, which was upon the waters of the river, when he held up his right hand and his left hand unto heaven, and sware by him that liveth for ever that it shall be for a time, times, and an half; and when he shall have accomplished to scatter the power of the holy people, all these things shall be finished. [8] And I heard, but I understood not: then said I, O my Lord, what shall be the end of these things? [9] And he said, Go thy way, Daniel: for the words are closed up and sealed till the time of the end. [10] Many shall be purified, and made white, and tried; but the wicked shall do wickedly: and none of the wicked shall understand; but the wise shall understand. [11] And from the time that the daily sacrifice shall be taken away, and the abomination that maketh desolate set up, there shall be a thousand two hundred and ninety days. [12] Blessed is he that waiteth, and cometh to the thousand three hundred and five and thirty days. [13] But go thou thy way till the end be: for thou shalt rest, and stand in thy lot at the end of the days.

The new age of Aquarius is upon us.

The 5th Dimension Age of Aquarius 1969

When the Moon is in the Seventh House, and Jupiter aligns with Mars
Then peace shall guide the planets, and love will steer the stars
This is the dawning of the Age of Aquarius . . .

※※※

Harmony and understanding
Sympathy and trust abounding
No more forces of derision
Golden living dreams of visions
Mystic crystal revelations
And the mind's true liberation

http://www.youtube.com/watch?v=kjxSCAalsBE

## Age of Aquarius

The Age of Aquarius is either the current or new age in the cycle of astrological ages. Each astrological age, resulting from very slow processional movement of the Earth's rotation, is approximately 2,150 years long on average.

**PRECESSIONAL MOVEMENT OF THE EARTH:** The Earth rotates once a day about its axis of rotation. This axis itself rotates slowly, completing a rotation in approximately 26,000 years.

## 2012—Rebooting the System

A MESSAGE FROM The Star Elders channeled by Aluna Joy Yaxk'in Wednesday, 29 February, 2012 www.AlunaJoy.

It is becoming clear now, regarding the energies of this year of 2012, that we have the critical point on our evolution. We all have been waiting for this time. This is our time. As old souls, incarnated and still ones un-manifested in this physical reality, we come at these precarious junction points, at the end/beginning of ages, because we absolutely love it.

Now you . . . that are already in physical form, you are having to deal with your rapidly morphing DNA and beyond that, adjust to the actual laws of nature that are changing right under your feet. You will feel like the carpet has been ripped out from under your feet. But remember . . . this is your time, and you came here for this time. SO MANY have come to experience this rapid evolution and rebooting of an entire system. Your body IS going with you. This has been the plan for eons. Atlantis was only a dress rehearsal, and we know that it didn't go so well. But you have all learned and grown through this age, and this time . . . is your time. We can see from NO TIME, and we can see that you have completed the job. You are victorious, and you are celebrating in the most extraordinary style. Hold this dream of victory as you pass through this year with all of its tidal waves of energy that are coming.

There is no doubt that your body will feel rocked and surprised by this year's energies. But your heart and inner truths are unshakable now. Rely on this inner truth when your body is telling you differently. No one will be immune to this process. There are going to be a lot of mixed signals in the outer world. Don't listen to them.

There will be medical experts out there telling you to drug yourself with anti-anxiety and anti-depressants meds. This won't help you as you are going to reboot anyway. Fighting the process will only make it less joyful. There will be well meaning alternative healers as well who will tell you to eat this, or do that. Again don't listen to them unless your heart is in full resonance with their suggestions. Everyone has a unique past that comes from your spiritual ancestors. We are not talking about your genetics; like who are your parents or grandparents. We are talking about your spiritual past. This is an akashic past that is much more potent than that of your genetic past. Listen to your heart, your core, your inner constant.

This is your orientation point in a world that is wobbling like an out of control gyroscope. Fighting the transformation at this point will only make it harder and less joyful. There is no escape. If you are in a body, you will re-boot and re-celebrate. Remember . . . this is great fun for your spirit and soul. This is why you came here.

In these coming waves, you are going to feel out of sorts and your body is going to give you weird issues that seem to come and go. You might feel like you need to hunker down and lay low for these shifts and changes; but we do not suggest this, although it is your free will to do whatever you want. Let us explain . . . You know when you sit in a chair too long, you get stiff. This is what will happen if you don't KEEP MOVING while these waves wash over you.

You will not find the answers you need while hiding in your home praying for solutions. The world is moving into a unified field of collective manifesting. You cannot do this by yourself. Pieces of your solution to this transformation are out in the world with other like-minded souls. All the pieces to this transformation are spread out among all of you. This is why you need like-minded ones around you. These waves are too large to surf alone. You must do this together.

There are going to be a lot of huge waves in 2012 that we will be surfing together. This is a good time to gather with like-minded soul family that live in a place that is centered in the heart and not from fear. Surround yourself with FEARLESS beings. We love the logo "NO FEAR" that you wear, because this is what we are asking you to BE now; FEARLESS and full of LOVE, TRUST, and a deep knowing that the big celebration is nearly upon you all.

The following are some of the energy waves that, at this point in our no time perspective, we expect may come to you. This does not mean that it will happen as we say here. The future is not real and can change at any moment as you evolve. There may be other waves that are coming as well that we do not see today as Aluna transcribes this for you.

The first wave will be on your Equinox. GATHER TOGETHER and celebrate this beginning wave of your great transformation. Equinox will bring a much needed balance in your world that will be necessary for what comes after this date. Balance yourselves in preparation as you will need this later. We can't say this strong enough. Please hear this, and do as your heart calls. This balance will be essential in the days to come.

From Aluna . . .

On March 21st, we will enter the Maya year of 2 KAN (Kiche long count) and 10 EB (Yucatan Haab count). 2 KAN is about balancing duality, but Kan can also bring up survival issues. I think this is why the Star Elder are speaking strongly about gathering together with like-minded souls, so your collective positive intent will soften the duality and the body issues that might raise survival issues. Negative and fearful friends and family, etc . . . will be toxic to you now.

The year of 10 EB is about the awakened human finally arriving and anchoring. We are finally going to put our feet down on a new foundation to a new world. 10 is all about manifesting in a real physical dimension. EB is about exuding outer peace, but inside there can be inner turmoil. The outer peace is our heart knowing and truth. The inner turmoil, fear, etc . . . that we have inside is the last of the old programming fading away. If we do not feed it, it will starve. Feed the Love, starve the fear.

The next large wave we see that you might experience profoundly is a total solar eclipse on May 20th.

In the path of this total solar eclipse, your dimension will begin an entire reboot of its operating system on your Earth. As the sun is blocked so perfectly by your moon, in this very still, no-time place, a new operation system will be created and uploaded into your body as well as your world, solar system and universe. Remember that this is a universal shift and recalibration . . . not just a planetary one. We are shifting with you, as well as ascended masters and angelic realms. We are all transforming together as ONE in unity. If you are in the path of the shadow of this eclipse, the download will be quicker, more complete and graceful.

You will become the living messengers for this new download for the rest of the world that did not have the luxury to travel into the eclipse path. This new operating system will begin to spread across the Earth over some time (a month or two). Again we strongly say, gather with fearless ones on the days surrounding this reboot. Gather with ones that come from the inner knowledge of Love, trust and truth that this transformation of our reality is already victorious.

Another large wave we see that you might experience profoundly is the June 6th Venus transit. For the last 8 years, your collective consciousness has been building a model for a unified, universal heart. This process began on the last Venus transit on June 8th, 2004. This new unified, universal heart model will be downloaded into the new operating system. The collective unified heart will be anchored. Any place where there is not love expressed, it will be shaken to its core. This will cover everything including your personal relationships all the way to global governmental systems. This new down load will make selfish acts nearly impossible to achieve. In other words, we will begin to think, act and live in the knowing that there is no separation and all life is connected. We will not be able to make a choice without considering the whole and future generations. This new heart model will take several weeks before it is fully anchored.

The universe is loving and kind and will allow this heart transformation download slowly so you can readjust with each daily heart pulse. Breathe . . . surround yourself with loving, positive, like-minded souls. This will make your heart transformation a joyful experience instead of a painful one. But we see that this will be somewhat uncomfortable for everyone to a certain extent, as this new heart program has never been experienced in a human form before.

This program has been long awaited by so many of you that already consider your actions and the future reproductions of these actions. Thank you for holding this space open for this program to down load. You are and will be successful.

The next big wave we see will be on November 13th . . . the second total solar eclipse Now that the heart model has been fully anchored into your new heart, as well as into your world and our universe, this eclipse will be quite important and very potent as it makes necessary adjustments based on our collective consciousness. This will make the universe self-justifying. What we are saying here is that anything that is still not in alignment with unified love will be reprogrammed to make adjustments for human error. This is not a judgment on humanity. But we know that holding a perfect love space in your wobbling world will be hard to accomplish 100% of the time. So the universe is giving you a break for any mis-qualified energy you may have anchored. We also tell you this to be easy on yourself.

It is difficult to hold perfect space in a radically morphing world. Relax and just be your truth as much as you can. The universe will clean up anything you might have done that came from anything but love. In this eclipse path, there will be a temporary no-time space in which to reboot all the upgrades. This eclipse will be quite intense, and we are glad that most of the passage of this eclipse is over the ocean to soften its impact.

During this time, we can see that there is going to be a lot of upgrading. Stay in a place of peace and neutrality as the reboot washes across the Earth. Now you are running on a fully upgraded and re-calibrated system. It is time to give this new world a test run. You have been ready for this for eons.

The next wave will come in mid-December on 12/12/12 which also falls on an important celebration day for the Maya 8 BATZ. For the Maya, this day is a recalibration of their sacred calendar, and it will set off an explosion that will light the fire under the new programming that we have helped download this entire year. Essentially the Maya

Elders will be plugging it ALL in. This comes almost 2 weeks before the December 21, 2012 date that so many of you are aware of.

The last wave of the year comes on December 21, 2012. All you old souls will be celebrating in love and peace. Any that have not allowed this recalibration to take place, and were strong enough to hold it off, will hit an extreme crisis point. Your job is to anchor love and positive intent in celebration, and THIS ACTION will bring these last hold outs into alignment with the new program. This is not a judgment for these souls. They were the last hold outs to keep the old world running up to the very last second, and they did this for us. This was a very hard job for them. ALL souls on your Earth are pieces of God. So don't forget this.

So, with this said, we suggest and hope that you will gather in HUGE numbers on December 21, 2012 around the Earth to celebrate no matter what the outer world is doing. Remember that you are living in the no-fear all-love zone. You are opening portals to your heart, the Earth and the universe. Be out on Mother Earth and under Father Sun. Go to your sacred sites, celebrate and be in love with all your soul family. This is your time. You have waited and prepared for a long time. So allow yourself to celebrate this victory and revel in the glory of the shining God that is in YOU and now anchored in the world and universe.

Be in Love and Peace and know all is well.

### *The Star Elders* http://spiritlibrary.com/spiritual-entities/the-star-elders

The Star Elders, a group of Cosmic Star Walkers, have come to Earth over and over and over again. They came to observe the cycles of Earth and wanted to know why Earth seemed to be out of sync with the rest of the Universe. If you ever felt totally alone, yet still felt there is something or someone else out there, this is why! We are just a bit out of sync with it so we can't see it yet. They fell in love with the people of Earth and decided to stay a while to teach what they knew. Everything was done in a sense of fun, ease and great humor.

The Star Elders have been coming here as early as prehistoric times. They have influenced eras we do not have memories of or historical account. They were here in the times of Atlantis and Lemuria, for the birth of Incan Worlds, at the birth of the Egyptian era, for the forming of the Himalayas in Tibet and when the belief system that Buddhism was built on came to be. They spent time on the sacred mountains in North America where the I AM master teaching sprung up from.

Anywhere a culture, religion or tradition seemed to spring up from nowhere fully developed, the Star Elders were a part of that evolutionary jump. They planted seeds of cosmic truth in different times and locations and let things evolve naturally. This is why we can discover common threads between beliefs and traditions in most ancient cultures. The foundations for these cultures came from the same source—from the people from the Stars, the Bird Tribes, the Star Walkers. How these truths developed into seemingly different cultures was at the whim of the local people, but the foundation of truth has remained even today.

The Star Elders are very much like the ascended masters we know of today. They work with the Great White Brotherhood (not based on the color of the skin or gender); Lord Meru and the Brotherhood of the 7 Rays; Archangel Michael and other Archangels; Jesus/Jesuha/Sananada/Christ; Mother Mary; Saint Francis; Buddha and a multitude of Hindu/Buddhist Masters, and the list goes on and on.

Now this sounds a bit far-fetched, but on the other side these guys all know each other and work together toward a common goal to empower humanity into mastery and to guide us through this shift of the ages that is upon us!

The last time the Star Elders were on Earth in physical form was about 800 years ago in an area we now called Guatemala in a site called Quirigua. They had finished measuring the new Earth land masses after huge changes in environment. These shifts happened over 10,400 years ago and still are the basis of our catastra-phobia of end times today. They had calculated the very complicated cycles of life on Earth and how they related to the Cosmos.

The Star Elders knew the Earth was about to enter a cosmic cocoon to be transformed from a worm into a butterfly. It was time for them to go. They could not be here for this process. We were on our own. They left and went back to the stars.

# PART II

# *Spirits Never Die*

**John 11:25** (KJV)
[25] Jesus said unto her, I am the resurrection, and the life: he that believeth in me, though he were dead, yet shall he live:

## Chapter 9

# LOVE, LOVE, LOVE

### *Universal Laws*

Your guides and angels can only help you if you ASK! They are right there—they have never left you, they are spirits just like you and are part of you. They were there when you were born and are waiting for you to talk to them. You have been sleeping. You are deaf and you are blind. You need to WAKE UP—it is time.

Can you imagine a stranger walking into your home and helping you with your laundry? Yes, it sounds pretty good to me, but most likely you would be somewhat apprehensive if a stranger just showed up without being asked. You need to connect with these strangers once again who are not really strangers; you have amnesia and they are there because you asked them to be. It was an agreement that they would always be there and ready and willing to help when you wake up.

In the spirit world, the one which you have forgotten who you really are and forgotten the other souls you know, there are "Universal Laws". You will soon be hearing more about these laws if you haven't already from many of the other old souls who have reincarnated to deliver messages to the masses ready to awaken from their long summer's sleep. ☺

It is a moment in time, a historical moment that has never happened in the galaxy! There has always been a multitude of spirits working with the many souls here on Earth and also in the galaxy. ☺ Some of you are not yet awake enough to know who you are and what is going on right NOW, but that is about to change.

Most nights when you sleep you are connecting to other dimensions. Some of you are very aware, some of you have been wondering, and some have not even given it a thought. Many are starting to get information, downloads and guidance—enough to have you searching for more. We have been separated from our spirit families for a very long time. We have been very busy creating and playing out our roles in order to be ready for this incredible time in history. The time has come—we are ready to move forward in our evolution in a very BIG way.

The "shift" of consciousness of the Earth and mankind is upon us. There are new energies—frequencies on our planet, in the Universe and galaxy that have been predicted for a very long time. You know things are different, and you are searching for information—information that will help you move with the changes.

Change is not easy; there are no shortcuts. Change is a process and is different for every single soul. If you don't change with the flow of the energy, things can get very difficult. If these words are resonating with you, then the time is now—The Kingdom of Heaven within The Holy Book of the Great Invisible Spirit.☺

There is no wrong and no right—**"Free Will and Choice" is the Universal Law** that states each soul must choose their own path and make their own choices. There is no one that can choose for you and you cannot choose for anyone else—not even your children. However, you can guide them and provide information. Their soul plan may have different choices than yours. I have been guilty more than once of doing the lessons of others. I have since given those lessons back so that they also may grow.

## LOSING LOVED ONES—MORE THAN MEETS THE EYES

A divine plan and divine timing unknown to either of us on this side of the invisible veil created our connection. We as spiritual beings masterfully arranged our meetings with others long before we entered this lifetime. As the plan unveils, it will become evident that there is much *more than meets the eyes.*

I participated in a play called "More Than Meets the Eye" and certainly not by coincidence since I had no intentions of playing any part.☺ This was one of those turning points in my life when I think back on it—a teacher becomes the student. Now the real test is before me as I play a new role on the grand stage of spiritual transformation. In the midst of writing this book, a terrible tragedy hit me hard and my entire house came tumbling down. His favorite band is Led Zeppelin and maybe he knew something deep down as he asked his best friend to play his favorite song when he was gone. ("Is", because he still is with us☺)

### "Ramble On"

Leaves are falling all around, It's time I was on my way.
Thanks to you, I'm much obliged for such a pleasant stay.
But now it's time for me to go. The autumn moon lights my way.
For now I smell the rain, and with it pain, and it's headed my way.
Sometimes I grow so tired, but I know I've got one thing I got to do . . .

**This book is dedicated to our beloved son, Michael**

*September 8th, 1977—September 11th, 2011* ☺

**Matthew 5:8** Blessed are the pure in heart: for they shall see God.

In this life, he was a Father, a Husband, a Son, a Brother, a Grandson, an Uncle, a Nephew, a Cousin and, most important, a FRIEND. His light shines bright as he is GUIDING us in ways you may or may not understand.

## *MICHAEL'S GIFT—GIFT IT FORWARD* ☺

In Michael's memory and in his honor, take time today and everyday to ☺ at someone and wait for that smile to be returned. Acknowledge that ☺ you just received and KNOW you have made someone smile. Every ☺ lights up another heart . . .

My beloved Michael ☺—my son, my teacher and my student—his light continues to shine bright as he guides the way. Michael was my grandmother in another life—her son was my father—my father had a twin brother.

During Michael's high school years, we decided to check out the local little theatre in our small community. Michael and his best friend were both interested in participating in other activities and we thought there just might be something interesting within the local little theatre. I was bent on Michael auditioning for a part in the play, thinking this would be great for his character and a wonderful life experience.

This is one of those times I now reflect upon as I step back and observe the outcome. When he was **not willing** to go up and audition, I thought that if I showed him how it was done then maybe he would go up and give it a go. Shaking like a leaf, I found some extra courage and managed to keep my nerves hidden during my audition. Of course, as a mother I wanted to set a good example by putting my heart and my soul into the scene.

It must have been the performance of a lifetime—I was offered the part! Not expecting this to happen, I was taken off guard and not sure if I should take on such an undertaking. At the end of the day, I accepted the new role on my path and found so many beautiful treasures to keep. I took on new experiences creating hair, makeup, clothing and playing the part, too! I must have looked like Wonder Woman or something! Who got the lesson there?

Michael was much more interested in the stage set up—lights, props, etc. Like they say, whoever is supposed to be there will show up and the play must go on!

So, you see, you may think you are making choices for the ones you love, but in reality, divine guidance will take the stage. Thank you, my dear Michael, for "showing me the way" over the many lifetimes we have shared. ☺ I love you!

That life experience was a brief display of the Universe letting me know that there is much "MORE THAN MEETS THE EYES"! It was taking on something you didn't think you would do and doing it because you knew it would help someone. This is exactly how I felt when I realized I would be writing this book—and not just a book, but a book about spirituality, a book about my *knowing* many of my past lives. I was stepping out into unknown territory again in this life, knowing it would be different this time.

I have done a lot of things over the years in this lifetime, but write a book was not on my list—although I had thought about it many times. What did I *know* about writing books and/or spirituality? What did I *know* about auditioning for a play and playing the part? Just because you haven't done it in this lifetime doesn't mean you haven't done it in another and it doesn't mean that you won't do it in this life. ☺ There isn't anything you can't do—that you haven't already done before.

One day of several thousand days, I was sitting at my computer digging through the Internet in search of anything I could get my head wrapped around that would help me out with the biggest quandary of my life. It had been seven months since I had found out who I was in my previous life, right down to a biography on the Internet and a book I co-wrote. I left that physical body the same year I was born into this life. I was a male with very little hair, had a wife, two sons and one son went missing in action in World War II, which I never got over.

As I was sitting there, a new acquaintance named Lydia called me. She was in Manchester, Connecticut, talking to Meg of Meg's Inspirationals. Meg, the owner of the store, asked her if she knew anyone who did reconnective healing? Immediately, Lydia thought of me because she had received a few healing sessions just a few weeks prior to this event. Lydia also mentioned a spiritual reader named Vanessa who just happened to be in the store that very day. It was as if by magic—an opportunity out of thin air emerged just when I needed it the most.

Lydia, a member of my soul family, played out her role on the grand stage of life just like a pro that day, just like we planned she would as she was chosen for this task to connect our lives. There were other possibilities and probabilities available if and when required.

*"Your mind does not know the way . . . your heart has already been there And, your soul has never left it. Follow your heart . . ."* **Lydia Shaughnessy Certified Angelic Essence Healer, Reiki Practitioner, RYT** www.angeleyesct.com

I always had questions. I was willing to get the answers however they should appear. And today the Universe heard my call, then returned the call and next thing I know, I'm having a meeting with Meg and getting the reading of a lifetime with Vanessa. I find it very comical NOW, thinking back. The spirits LOVE it when a plan comes together. ☺

I had questions, of course, that would save me eons and eons of time.

Upon entering the room, Vanessa was overwhelmed by all of them (the angels and guides) being so excited to see me. She asked me if this was the first time I had received a reading of sorts, or had it been a long time since I received a reading? I laughed and said, "No, but I have never had a reading with you." ☺ She went on to say that they were so excited that I was there and that they wanted me to know that my being there was not a coincidence. I laughed again and said, "I had a feeling you would say that!" I seemed to "know" what she was going to say—but I didn't know HOW I knew.

During the reading, I mentioned to her that I found myself often giving advice during conversations with people and, most recently, during or after I AM giving a healing session. I felt in some strange way that the information did not come from me because the words that came out of my mouth seemed to be from someone who was educated in psychology or physiology. I went on to say how I would end the conversation with my clients, stating, "I am not sure where all of that information came from, but it sounded really good—so if you liked it, then, hey, just go with it."

## THERE ARE NO COINCIDENCES

Let's talk a minute here to analyze my meeting with Vanessa. When I stop to think about it, the details are outstanding.

1) I had to live in Connecticut.

2) I had to live in the area of Manchester.

3) I had to become a reconnective healing practitioner.

4) I had to meet Lydia by chance at her old job at Staples.

5) A person named Linda had to want and need a healing, then search for a reconnective healing practitioner at Meg's.

6) Lydia had to get the job that she just got to go into Meg's to sell advertising.

7) I had to be ready, willing and open!

8) Many, many details in between these lines were also played out in the scenes.

Imagine the bigger picture and all of the scenes that played out. There certainly had to be several rehearsals before the "BIG SHOW". ☐ This is an example of one small detail of a much greater divine plan that we all have a part in. If any of these events had not occurred, there would have been different ones put down in front of me—a different set of possibilities and probabilities set up for a different circumstance.

The Universe is always trying to give us messages. Depending where you are on the path depends on how well you are receiving the information. Your spirit guides and angels will knock down chairs and throw snowballs at you if they have to get your attention. Hopefully, you will make it easy on them—pay attention. The spirits know everything you're thinking! ☺

I was in training for Level III reconnective healing qualifications when the instructor held three minutes of silence for all of us to stop and reflect on what circumstances and/or events had to take place that brought us to that training in Rhode Island. I was laying down on one of the healing tables with my eyes closed when all of a sudden I was tickled! I giggled out loud and quickly opened my eyes, thinking WHO would do this to me during the three minutes of **silence**? My partners, who were not standing anywhere near the table, looked at me while holding their hands over their mouths and shaking their heads in dismay! It was spirit letting me KNOW. ☺

Upon discovering I was an orthopedic surgeon in my previous life, I had two questions: 1) How did I know this? 2) Why did I know this? Talk about sleeping at the realm. ☺

**I AM CLAIRSENTIENCE**—a knowing, psychic knowing, inner knowing. I always knew that I knew things, things that I had no idea I could know about. I had no idea I had a psychic ability, which explains a whole lot of unexplainable details. This ability and other gifts and abilities are there waiting for you to claim. You have always had them. You brought them with you—from other lifetimes—in your DNA!

It is The Kingdom of Heaven within The Holy Book of The Great Invisible Spirit☺. Are you ready to claim your spirituality?

What is clairsentience or paranormal knowing? Other names include being a clairsentient, clair knowing, clair sensing, psychic knowing, having a knowing, (sometimes) inner knowing.

Clairsentience is used both for paranormal feeling and paranormal knowing. With paranormal knowing, the person gets an answer. With this answer, he got the feeling/knowing to be absolutely sure the answer is correct, without being able to give a rational explanation.

The (clair) knowing perhaps seems to come from nowhere—it doesn't come from a feeling or intuition, but comes from "nowhere", so it seems. When a person is pure and doesn't influence the answers, he gets objective answers. But impurity or influencing can deform the answers. A person with clairsentience abilities doesn't get the answer from his/herself, but from a cosmic source of information. The things the person gets aren't words or images at first, but a universal energy that the person then translates to his/her world in his/her language of images. The translation happens without thinking of the person and happens automatically, unless there isn't any word for it or it can't be imagined. When there does exist words (with the right nuances) or images for what it can be translated to, the person gets this through before he thinks about the answer or what the answer might be. Often during phrasing the question, the answer already gets through.

Exactly—right on the money! Who KNEW? Clairsentience is one of the most interesting aspects of the psychic world. This ability covers a number of things, such as the ability to read people and their physical state, which explains why I can read souls.

Having a tingling or tickling sensation on the skin, face or hands, or having the hair on the back of your neck stand up when you are being touched by spirit are some of the sensations you may feel☺

This ability is essential for healers and counselors, therapists and anyone who works with people, especially psychics and spiritual advisors and interpreters☺.

We are all born with a psychic ability. Through our experiences, we build up walls against the world and lose our ability to use our special sense of others' spirits and get out of touch with our own. Our consciousness loses the ability to control its spiritual gifts and abilities. Later, we can restore this ability through life-altering experiences or through development of our spirituality—The Kingdom of Heaven within The Holy Book of The Great Invisible Spirit☺.

This is exactly what happened to me. It came from nowhere; it came into me out of thin air! This projection of the senses or feeling of other people's energies can be an amazing gift to have.

Clairsentience is a complex psychic ability. One of the most interesting things about clairsentience is that it is the gift that is most often ignored, or not even noticed by those that have it. Certainly, I had no idea I had this gift. Now, with the new energies on Earth, the spirits have been guiding me to discovering my abilities right on time, on schedule to write this book for you.

That answers the first question *of "****HOW*** *do I know"* what I *know*. Getting that information was hard for me to wrap my head around at first, but when I got it, all the "lights" came on and OH WHAT A FEELING, A GREAT FEELING IT IS—liberating indeed!

Chances are the lights are starting to come on for you, too? If you want your lights to come on, just say "YES"! Your pure, sincere intention is all it takes to get started on your path.

Now that the **"HOW"** I *know* what I know was taking on the new energies, the second question was already starting to unveil☺.

## *"WHY did I know what I know?"*

A very loaded question!

Not all questions can be answered without learning the lessons first. Find the gift in the pain—pain and suffering are motivators—give thanks and offer forgiveness.

There would be a series of teachers, guides and angels put on my path—ready, willing, and able to assist me just as I needed them☺. I thought I would ask the question and a logical answer would be given.

## THE SOUL KNOWS

> *"When the student is ready, the master appears."*
> **—Buddhist proverb**

Along my journey, I discovered many of my soul family who were here on Earth playing in other roles during some of the same periods of time when I was here before. Many of these lifetimes were during the time of Jesus and other major historical events.

You will soon come to know your soul family, too. One of my soul sisters was Paul the Apostle in another life and also my younger brother in another. I was the 11$^{th}$ son born of the 12 sons. We had the same mother—the other 10 brothers had a different mother. Our mother died giving birth to my youngest brother. The older 10 brothers sold me to slavery, unknown to my father.

I knew I was very spiritual and I knew that I wasn't religious in a church-going way. I despised all of the hate and war over religion and I made a clear distinction early on. There is a reason for everything and we are all working the magical kingdom together. We need to forgive those who have trespassed against us—an important part of clearing yourself toward your spiritual transformation.

We are all spiritual beings having a human experience—we are ONE. The Creator God created "All That Is". We are "God sparks"—when we connect, we are united and become one with our Creator☺.

I believe in God and always have. I believe in angels and spirit guides. I believe many ascended masters who have walked this Earth have reincarnated into this lifetime. I also believe that you don't have to go to church to find heaven. The Kingdom of Heaven is within The Holy Book of The Great Invisible Spirit☺.

Some people said my father would not go to heaven because he didn't believe in "God"! Many of these same people believed going to church cleansed their sins and they were ready to go back into the world and do it all over again. Attending class doesn't give you an automatic pass. You must do the work.

As a human in his last life, my father had his share of life experiences and stinky roses. We all have our crosses to bear. The lessons we have created before we incarnate are not always pleasant. If you don't experience the unpleasant, you will not learn to experience the pleasant. Understand and acknowledge the lesson and let it go if it no longer serves you. If you feel pain, acknowledge the feeling, take it into your soul, then let it go because it no longer belongs to you. Alter and shift your vibration to the next level.

My father has a **heart of gold**—a good heart, a loving heart, a heart that cared for everyone and anything around him. He brought it with him—his personality from lifetime to lifetime. He was my father in this lifetime, he who had many daughters; he was my mother in another lifetime, he who had many sons. I was his third daughter born in this lifetime; I was his third-born son in the other lifetime. It's a balancing of karma, a return to full circle for a new cycle.

If he had it, he gave it. He has given his last cent out of his pocket and he worked very hard for his money, sometimes held down three jobs. He would give the shirt off his back. He is very generous—he is my father and I love him.

By choice, he came into this life because he was the most likely to accomplish the task that would help the rest of us. He rejoices now as he sees the fruits of his garden come to life—and he loved his garden! He worked up the ground, making it clean and clear every year. He planted the seeds and harvested the crop. His spirit left his body several years ago, yet the tree still bears fruit and this year, the year of 2012, will be his best year yet! If you mind your garden, you will have abundance forever.

As tough as the times were sometimes to be his daughter, there was a reason for every season. I am certain it was very tough at times for him to be my father and the father of five girls in this day and age. If it were not for him—him who was my mother in another life—you wouldn't be reading this book right now, which he planned in advance with you for you.

## The Angels Came—The Room Filled with A Glorious Light

He suffered many years from congestive heart failure. He did his share of drinking and smoking, not exactly taking care of his tent. We knew each time he got hit with the heart failure that the next time might kill him. In fact, the first one almost did. You see what he had to go through to make this all come together?

My mother called me very early in the morning on a cold and snowy February day. She said, "Dad is going to the hospital. He couldn't breathe and he finally let me call 911." By the time I got to the house, he had already left with the ambulance. My mother said the paramedics said not to rush to the hospital—come whenever you can.

My mother had a crippling disease that kept her from doing the things most of us take for granted. She had the same disease in another lifetime—she was my father in that lifetime and her companion was my father from this lifetime, who was my mother in that lifetime—both are very old souls. ☺

She had a pin in one hip and the other hip was plastic. She also had a plastic knee. There was water on the floor brought in with the paramedics from the snow outside. I didn't want my mother to slip and fall like she did when she was pregnant with me.

When I arrived at the hospital, the nurses and doctors asked, "Where is your mother?" I explained that she didn't go out much because of her lack of mobility. They said, "Go NOW, get your mother! We are losing him." This is not what I expected at all! I went over to my father and said, "Dad, I love you. Please hang on! I am leaving now to get Mom." I rushed out the door and while driving, I thought, "Oh my God! I never ever thought it would come down to this. I never ever thought that I would be standing there with just my mother and I."

I had no time to call the other four sisters at this point in time. I didn't know how I would tell my mother that she needed to come with me. I prayed to God, Mother Mary and all of my angels to please help me now. I pleaded with them to protect him and help him pull through. I remember how strong my mother was that dreadful day and how strong I wasn't. (I have a feeling she knew more than I did then about all of this.) There wasn't much time—my mother had difficulty just getting into a car! We arrive at the hospital and rushed into the Emergency Room, not knowing what to expect. The doctors were amazed—he made it through☺.

He became weaker and weaker each time he had congestive heart failure. It was four years later when he had number 12 and a few weeks later when he began his journey home. He did not believe in anything—not even God! I said to my father two weeks before his departure, "Dad, please remember when the angels come, they are going to help you get where you need to go. Dad, please promise me. Dad, listen to them—they are here to help you." Then he said, "Oh thank you, sweetie. There is no problem—I can do this myself."

The day before his passing, I asked him, "Dad, have any of those angels come by that I told you about?" He said, "Yes honey, they have, but I told you I can do this myself." It was typical of what you'd hear from a stubborn, hard-working European man!

*"As Adam falls sick and is in pain, all his sons and daughters came to him, and he briefly recounts to them the story of the Fall. Seth and Eve travel to the doors of the Garden to beg for some oil of the tree of mercy* [i.e., the Tree of Life]. *On the way Seth is attacked and bitten by a wild beast, which goes away when ordered by Seth. Michael refuses to give them the oil at that time, but promises to give it at the end of time, when all flesh will be raised up, the delights of paradise will be given to the holy people and God will be in their midst."* http://en.wikipedia.org/wiki/Life_of_Adam_and_Eve

On that last day with his wife and daughters all around him, he told us, "I am going home at 6 o'clock." It is true—we even pick the time we are going home. We create before we incarnate every single detail right down to the last second. However, he failed to mention to us that day whether it would be 6 p.m. or 6 a.m. ☺

So when 6 p.m. passed on by, I **knew** the next morning he was going home. I called the hospital at 5:30 a.m. to ask about his condition. I was surprised and relieved when they said nothing had changed. Just before my husband and I left the house at 6:04 a.m., the phone rang. The nurse was calling from the hospital and said his breathing had changed. I knew Dad was heading on home. ☺

When we arrived, one of my brothers-in-law had been there all night. I sat down beside my father. I took his hand; it was icy and stiffness was starting to set in from the lack of oxygen. His eyes were closed, his breathing was shallow.

I sat quietly holding his hand, and then I knew the angels were now ready to take him home to the heavens. I said to my father, *"Dad, the angels are here. They are ready to take you to see your kitty cats on the other side. Please Dad, they are holding the light to show you the way."* The soul truly knows.

Then suddenly, one of his eyebrows arched as if in surprise! He took one last big breath and was gone—he left his body! The room filled with a beautiful light that came in and crawled around one side of the room until the entire room was filled with a glorious light! YES, that glorious light we keep hearing about. I stood immersed in it—seeing the light, feeling the glory and the unconditional LOVE!

*"But do thou, Seth, go to thy father Adam, since the time of his life is fulfilled. Six days hence, his soul shall go off his body and when it shall have gone out, thou shalt see great marvels in the heaven and in the Earth and the luminaries of heaven. With these words, straightway Michael departed from Seth."—http://en.wikipedia.org/wiki/Life_of_Adam_and_Eve*

The light stayed for about 30 minutes and then left the room the same way it came into the room. You know what you know—my husband and my brother-in-law knew it, too. He went to the light and met up with other souls he knew. He did his life review as we all do. He also came to terms with all his experiences in this life and then returned to his soul state.

## *I AM*

> *"I think therefore I AM."*—**Rene Descartes (1595-1650)**

Yes **I AM** spiritual, but I didn't realize that I KNEW anything about the subject. My quest for an answer to my second question—WHY did I know who I was in the previous lifetime including all the details— became a full-time enlightened endeavor. I began to weave the pieces together.

I spent hours researching everything from spirituality, past lives and reincarnation. My guides and angels once told me during a reading with Vanessa that I spent 25 hours a day searching on the Internet. That was no exaggeration! They knew everything about me—they knew what I was going to say before I said it!

When I registered to attend a healing/ health expo in the state of Massachusetts, I signed up to take in some of the presentations on various topics and one of them had me wondering if I should be attending. I was getting a feeling, a knowing that something wasn't right. I asked Vanessa to ask spirit a question that I was trying to ask about the presentation and about my feeling, but I couldn't remember the name of it. It was on the tip of my tongue but not even a clue would come through. Then out of the blue, Vanessa blurted, "Rings of Odem." I looked at her and I said, "Oh my God, they told you that?!"

She burst out laughing! She laughed till she cried while I sat there in bewilderment. I mean, I *knew* that they were real and that the information I was getting was crazy, right. I knew that there was no way anybody could know the stuff Vanessa was telling me. But, I didn't know they knew me so well—that they knew I was concerned about this presentation AND that they knew the exact name of it! They knew what was on my mind!

Like I said, everything happens for a reason. If that didn't happen, I wouldn't be writing about it now in this book to tell you. Spirit let me know I needed to attend because there was something there I needed to learn, something to put in my pocket and keep it a while. That little something turned out to be discernment. The guides, angels and ascended masters wanted me to understand sometimes there is some grey matter weaving throughout some of the "Truth". When we are searching for answers, we must become aware of truth versus fiction. Yet, there is always some sort of truth mixed in with the false claims. If you don't know already, you will soon learn how to recognize the difference as you move throughout the levels on your path. Wherever you are on your path is exactly where you are supposed to be.

And that's exactly why they constantly put treasures on our paths. One of the most important things that they said to me during that first reading at the time had no meaning to me whatsoever. Vanessa had given me a name and said to me, "Remember this *name* and mark my words, this is important." I remember thinking how strange it was that this *name* was given to me as being so very important, but I didn't have the foggiest idea of what it was about. Of course, I tried really hard to remember and for the *life* of me, I could not remember the name she gave me that day. They knew that I would not remember— and they also knew me so well—they knew that I would search the ends of the Universe to remember. It was on the list of possibilities and probabilities that was created by all of us before I reincarnated into this life.

There was a strong probability that I would get the information I needed to answer the "WHY" question while I was reaching for the stars for the answers.

## *REACHING FOR THE STARS*

*"The road of life twists and turns and no two directions are ever the same. Yet our lessons come from the journey, not the destination."—* **Don Williams Jr.** *(American novelist **and poet, b. 1968)***

It sounded like a name that you would hear in the Bible, I remembered. It was hard for me to remember, because even though I spent my very young years searching for God, Mother Mary and all of the angels, by the time I got to high school at around the age of 14, I was not spending any time in a church. Regardless of how many times I asked in all of the readings with Vanessa after the first one, they would not repeat the name they gave to me. It was frustrating and I wondered why they wouldn't repeat the name? Remember, there is a reason for everything.

Upon contemplation, I realized it was part of the plan so that I would dig deeper to gain information that I needed. Of course, trying too hard, I have come to learn, is another signal. The more you allow the information to come to you, the more information will come to you. It is all about trust and faith and being a clear channel. If it is meant for you to get the information—**if your heart is in the right place** and you are open to receiving it—then trust it will be given.

As I became "enlightened", I started to remember things that happened to me when I was younger. I was a small child who was wandering down a dusty dirt road looking for God. My mother was in a body cast after having surgery on her hip. She had fallen when she was pregnant with me. I remembered I was sick and a man carried me home. This happened at least twice. I asked my mother many times over my life who this man was. She always slid it off and said, "I don't know, honey." Today I do KNOW—I was carried home by an angel.☺

## SPIRITUAL BEINGS

### *We are spiritual beings having a human experience*☺

*"You are a shimmering burst of spiral hallelujahs that has temporarily taken on the form of a human being, agreeing to endure amnesia about your true origins. And why did you do that? Because it was the best way to forget the exquisitely unique and robust identity that would make you such an elemental force in our 14-billion-year campaign to bring heaven all the way down to Earth."*—**Rob Brezsny**

If they want your attention and need to get you to be somewhere to receive what you will need, then it will happen because it was part of the plan you created with them. Understand how very close and connected they are to you—they are part of you. The guides and angels and ascended masters were again very, very clear on making this point when they demonstrated by giving me information that was on the tip of my tongue. The words were still in my brain somewhere—not even in my mind because I could not remember them (very odd, don't you think, for a soul who knows?).

Every single detail of how the game is played is carefully planned so that we will follow the next lead. I knew that name had something to do with the title of my book, but what? They knew that it would be presented to me just at the right time and at the right place. I can still remember the day when it happened. It was a magical spiritual event!

I was at my doctor's office back home in Canada about two months after my son Michael crossed over to the other side. I was sitting in an examination room, waiting for the doctor. As I waited, I was looking around the room. I saw a picture on the wall of "**ELIJAH with the Widow from Zarephath**".

I had no idea, not even a clue, about the story behind the picture that day. That picture had energy; it was very powerful and I could feel the information it was starting to give me.

**Ecclesiastes 3 (KJV)**
¹*To every thing there is a season, and a time to every purpose under the heaven*

There was absolutely no doubt in my mind. I *knew* right away the name I had forgotten was **"ELIJAH"**—the same name most of you have also forgotten and not in the same way I had forgotten. It wasn't just the name **"ELIJAH"** that spirit wanted me to know. Spirit wanted me to know about the story behind the picture so that I could remember him not only for myself, but for "olive" us.

If they were trying to cause me pain, they were doing a very good job of it! I knew I was on to something, but yet I couldn't quite put my finger on it!

# Chapter 11

# OLD SOULS

## *ELIJAH*

The picture on the wall was **"ELIJAH" with the "WIDOW OF ZAREPHATH"** as seen exactly below from Wikipedia, the free encyclopedia.

### Prophet Elijah

*Elijah reviving the Son of the Widow of Zarephath* by Louis Hersent

*Matthew 17:11-12*
*¹¹And Jesus answered and said unto them, Elias truly shall first come, and restore all things. ¹²But I say unto you, That Elias is come already, and they knew him not, but have done unto him whatsoever they listed. Likewise shall also the Son of man suffer of them.*

Elijah has reincarnated many times before. He <u>was not</u> John the Baptist. Elijah was the cousin of John the Baptist during that time in history.

## His name was JESUS

According to Wikepedia, in the Gospel of Luke, Herod Antipas hears some of the stories surrounding Jesus. Some tell Herod that John the Baptist, whom he had executed, has come back to life. Others tell him that it is Elijah. Later in the same gospel, Jesus asks his disciples who the people say that he is. The apostles' answers included Elijah, among others.

However, Jesus' ministry had little in common with that of Elijah; in particular, he preached the forgiveness of one's enemies, while Elijah killed his. Miracle stories similar to those of Elijah were associated with Jesus (e.g., raising of the dead, miraculous feeding). Jesus implicitly separates himself from Elijah when he rebukes James and John for desiring to call down fire upon an unwelcoming Samaritan village in a similar manner to Elijah. Likewise, Jesus rebukes a potential follower who wanted first to return home to say farewell to his family, whereas Elijah permitted this of his replacement Elisha.

We play different roles each time we incarnate, although our purpose remains the same. When we return to the other side of the veil in pure spirit form, each time having left our physical body, we undergo a life review with other spirits who are our soul family. Over our many lifetimes in the physical body, we have created sets of possibilities and probabilities that will assist us while in physical form to connect with our spirit form. Many times our lessons in the next life are the exact opposite of a lesson in a previous life. I don't mean to sound like a broken record—even the fact that I repeat this over and over again—THERE IS REASON FOR EVERYTHING.

The spirit or soul of Elijah, Jesus and many others are one of the same who had life experiences opposite of the life experiences created before, yet aiming for the same goal. It's a balancing act of yin and yang and of karma—creating energy that creates life itself—without it, there would be no purpose and no life. It is an energy that makes the world, the Universe and the galaxy go round and round. A nonlinear energy is created of our individual DNA blueprint using all of the elements of our spiritual experiences throughout all of the periods of time. As each and every soul is fulfilling their life purposes, they are striving to complete their individual soul purpose. Let's bring Jacob home.

*Heaven above, heaven below;*
*stars above, stars below;*
*all that is above, thus also below;*
*understand this and be blessed.*

**—Kircher, Prodrom. Copt., pp. 193 and 275**

There is a well-known saying that applies perfectly: "Opposites attract." Likewise, like charges repel. Positive charges and negative charges will attract each other and come together. Two positive or two negative charges will push each other away.

Our lifetimes are like particles that act together and become a system like "quantum entanglement". They behave like one spirit, but remain separate in body and soul. They sit on the same teeter-totter, no matter how long the seesaw is, even if it is one million miles long or dimensions apart. When the third-dimensional, very dense energy is lifted, there is an opportunity to connect and become more—reconnecting to our spiritual selves.

Our Mother, the Earth, has reincarnated into fifth-dimensional energies and we as great masters have come together as "ONE" with our "SOURCE", living life in our physical bodies on Earth in paradise or heaven.

**Quantum entanglement** is the name given to the things that a pair of particles do. Sometimes, two particles will act together and become a system. They behave like one object, but remain two separate objects. No matter how long the seesaw is, even if it is one million miles long, if one end is down then the other end must be up, and this happens instantly.

Along with many other elements, the four classical elements of earth, water, air and fire are used in our spiritual transformation.

## *The Power and Majesty of The Elements*

Ronna Herman, internationally known author and messenger for Archangel Michael. www.RonnaStar.com * Email: RonnaStar@earthlink.net

Thursday, 1 March, 2012 (posted 15 March, 2012)

Beloved masters, an understanding of the elements of **FIRE, AIR, WATER,** and **EARTH,** which are unique components, facets or elements of the nature of our Father/Mother God within this Sub-universal experience, is vitally important as you seek greater wisdom and Self-Mastery. These are the four major elements which were encoded within the bodily system of the original human form to assist in Self-realization and Self-mastery on the material plane of existence. These elements are supplied to all created matter in this Sub-Universe via the great Archangels' RAY-diation of the twelve Rays of God Consciousness from the Heart Core Essence of our Father/Mother God.

*** The Etheric Body and Soul Self are attuned to and fed by the Element of COSMIC FIRE.**

*** The Mental Body resonates to and is energized by the Element of AIR /ETHER**

*** The Emotional Body is attuned to and affected by the Element of WATER.**

*** The Physical Body is anchored by and attuned to the Element of EARTH for the duration of each Soul's journey into the realms of density, the first through the fourth dimensions.**

The qualities, attributes and virtues of the Seven Rays of God Consciousness for this solar system were placed within Spheres of Light. These spheres, known as chakras, were designed to spin at a very high velocity, which made them appear to be spinning cones of Light radiating from the front and back of the physical body. Therefore, you are constantly radiating frequencies of Light out into the world of form. The power of the vibrational patterns, as well as the frequency level of the harmonics you project, will determine whether you will experience joy, peace and abundance, or limitation, stress and discord. Every living cell within your body is a capacitor which stores memories and energy patterns. For every feeling there are ***endocrine glands secretions*** produced which match the vibrational patterns you emit. Therefore, you might say that there is a specific energy pattern of hate and an energy pattern of love, and so on in varying degrees, depending on the power, force and consistency of the energy you project.

As you begin the journey of ascension back into the realms of Light, you gradually lose density within the physical vessel—not necessarily body mass—but your bodily form begins to resonate with higher and higher frequencies of Light. Never before have so many masters of Light walked the Earth among the masses. Many brave Souls were given the option of leaving the planet and continuing their work/mission from within the Celestial Cities of Light, or to continue their service to humankind within the framework of their chosen earthly environment. We wish you all to know that we are well-pleased with those of you, the Light Bearers, who are steadfastly walking through the dense, shadowed valleys of darkness in order to create a pathway of Light for others to follow.

Gaining mastery of the four elements of God-consciousness will assist you in creating a constant flow of **Sacred Fire** energy throughout the chakra system and the physical vessel. The Etheric Body vehicle is composed of the ***ELEMENT OF FIRE***. In the beginning phase of your ascension process, the more refined vibrational frequencies of God-consciousness must first filter through the Etheric Body before they gradually begin to flow freely throughout the physical vessel. You must slowly build up a tolerance for these refined frequencies of God Light so that they do not create too much discomfort or do bodily harm. The Sacred Fire energy, Adamantine Particles, must flow through the Heart Chakra first, in order to be activated by your loving intention, before this Elixir of Life can freely flow throughout the body. Gradually, over time, as the frequencies of your Soul Song become more refined, you will be able to magnetize higher levels of Cosmic energy as well as greater quantities of Adamantine Particles of Light.

The ***AIR ELEMENT*** focuses on the Mental Body, the plane of mental consciousness. The mental nature is fueled by the Sacred Breath of God Consciousness. That is why the breathing techniques you have been given are so important. Soul-awareness is the critical beginning phase of awakening to one's Divine Nature. The Third Eye, the Pineal and Pituitary Glands, and the Sacred Mind are all critical components of the Mental Body.

The Emotional Body is fueled via the ***ELEMENT OF WATER***. The Mental Body provides the seed thoughts and the Emotional Body fuels the ***E-motion or energy in motion***. As we have often explained, your creations are either a product of the ego desire-body or the desires and inspiration of the Soul. The Throat and the Solar Plexus are integral power sources for the Emotional Body. However, the full power of manifestation begins when you have tapped into the Kundalini Sacred Fire or the Adamantine Particles of God Light stored within the Root

Chakra, and you have completed the connection with your Soul Star and OverSoul Self so that you have access to the Antakarana, River of Life. The activation and harmonization of the Mental and Emotional Bodies and the merging of the lower and upper chakras via the Heart Chakra result in a merger of the Father God and Mother Goddess qualities, virtues and abilities within the physical vessel. Your level of **godliness** is predicated on the harmonic resonance of your Soul Song, or the dimensional levels in which you are attuned.

The ***ELEMENT OF EARTH*** via the physical vessel is both an anchor and your means of soaring into the realms of Light once more. You cannot ignore the physical vessel and still fulfill your earthly mission. If you deny the bodily form, you are denying your God-given uniqueness and the specific, complex form that you chose for this life's journey into the material realm of existence. You, along with the guidance of your guardian angels and your Council of Light, chose the appropriate DNA /ancestral lineage, the race, culture and circumstances you would be born into for this specific life's experience. A broad spectrum of tests, challenges and opportunities were programmed to give you the best opportunity for Soul-growth. These events were designed to be initiated at the appropriate times throughout your lifetime. As always, free will applies, and it is up to each person as to how he/she handles the tests and takes advantage of the opportunities. Do you understand that each and every person is constantly releasing or emitting energy which originated from the God Source? You are using this God-given gift of Light/Life in either a positive or a negative manner. Via your free will, you are the cocreator, the builder of your own reality.

Many of you are experiencing a transformation process of ascending in consciousness along with physical evolution whereby the Kundalini Fire stored within the Root Chakra is moving swiftly up the chakra system and throughout the physical vessel. This too is a dynamic and vital part of the ascension process. We have asked our messenger to share with you an article which was prepared for one of her recent wisdom teachings webinar classes:

## Kundalini * Serpent Fire

**Fire Of God, Sacred Fire, Sacred White Fire And Kundalini Fire Are All Terms Used For Adamantine Particles Of Light, The Fuel Of Life Breathed Forth From The Heart Core Of The Supreme Creator.**

**KUNDALINI:** A Sanskrit word which literally means **coiled**. This Sacred God Fire lies coiled at the base of the spine, and until activated, it is dormant or at rest and unconscious. It is often envisioned as a sleeping serpent; hence a number of English renderings have been created using terms such as "***serpent power.***" The ancients tell us that the Kundalini resides within the Root Chakra at the base of the spine in three and a half coils. It has been described as a residual/ reserve source of pure **God Fire**. According to ancient wisdom teachings, there are two nerve currents in the spinal column, a coiled double helix within a hollow tube, sometimes called a "Rod of Power," that runs along in front of the spinal column. The **Caduceus** symbol, used as a healer's and a medical symbol, is an ancient drawing of two entwined serpents around a central rod with wings at the top. You may see this symbol on Wikipedia: http://en.wikipedia.org/wiki/Caduceus

Through meditation and various other spiritual practices, the Kundalini is awakened and will begin to rise up through the chakra system alongside the spine. The progression of **Kundalini fire** through the different chakras leads to different levels of awakening and mystical experiences. When the Kundalini fire finally reaches the top of the head, the crown chakra, it sometimes produces a unique mystical experience as you are reconnected to the multiple facets of your Higher Self.

**THE FIRST MAJOR ACTIVATION** is usually felt in the back of the body between the shoulder blades. You will feel a pressure in that area, which can sometimes be quite uncomfortable. This is an indication that the back portal of your Sacred Heart is opening. I have often said, "**When this happens, we are growing our angel wings.**"

**THE SECOND ACTIVATION:** The Kundalini Fire rises to the top of the spine where it connects to the **Medulla Oblongata**, sometimes called "***The Mouth of God***." This is an indication that the ascension chakra is being activated. This activation will also affect the throat chakra. Practicing the Infinity Breath and toning will accelerate this process as they will help to break through any distorted energy blocks along the spinal column and within the chakra system. The throat chakra is one of the critical areas within the body which can cause distress as we strive to reclaim our personal power via the means of spoken language.

**THE THIRD ACTIVATION:** The Pineal and Pituitary Glands are stimulated and will begin to send impulses to the portal opening of the Sacred Mind so that full access to your personal temple of wisdom is realized. In addition, a firm reconnection with your Soul Star and **Over Soul-Higher Self** is established. When this is accomplished, your spiritual journey back into the higher realms will truly begin. Also at this point you are ready to receive the **Sacred Fire of Spirit; *Adamantine Particles of Creator Light will automatically begin to course into your Sacred Heart with every breath***. The driving-upward force of Serpent Fire is now accompanied by a down-pouring of Adamantine Particles via your **OverSoul-Higher Self,** which resides within your Soul Star. You must activate these particles of Creator Light with your loving intention as they course throughout your physical vessel, with the remainder flowing down into the Earth and out into the world for the benefit of the Earth and all humanity. As the Kundalini, Sacred Fire, begins to rise up your spinal column (the etheric tube of Light), you may experience times of intense inner heat while your exterior body will feel cold and perhaps even clammy. That is the reason why, initially, it is best to strive for a gradual release of the Kundalini Fire stored within the Root chakra so that you may slowly become acclimated to the integration of higher and higher frequencies of God Light.

*Remember, dear friends, faster and more is not necessarily better when you are in the midst of the transformational process of ascension. As a Self-master, you will begin to experience a constant uprising flow of inner Sacred Fire along with a downward thrust of Divinely encoded Spiritual Fire. This process will spur you on to a greater, expanded awareness, more inspired thought and the activation of capabilities of which you were not even aware. Bounteous blessings, miracles and assistance from our friends of the higher realms will become the norm, and you will be given an opportunity to become an active, full-fledged World Server along with the great multitude of World Servers from all over the planet. I, for one, am excited about what the future holds for us, the Bearers of Light. My mantra for 2012 is: THIS IS OUR YEAR TO SHINE! Eternal Love and angel blessings, Ronna*

Beloved masters, it is important that you realize that each phase of the Divine Plan is holographically imprinted upon the Earth's auric field, just as there are Memory Codes and impulses which have been or will be ignited within each of you at the appropriate time. No matter your beliefs, the celestial winds of change are growing stronger and stronger as they permeate everything and everyone on Earth. All must evolve or devolve; nothing can remain static. We encourage you to take advantage of the unprecedented opportunities which are constantly being offered to you. Know that we are with you every step of the way, onward and upward.

You are loved most profoundly,

I AM Archangel Michael.

*Chapter 999*

# LIFE CHANGING

### *Transfiguration—A Change that Glorifies or Exalts*

Transfiguration is a complete change of form or appearance into a more beautiful or spiritual state. Christ's appearance in radiant glory to three of his disciples

**Matthew 17:2 (KJV)**
*²And was transfigured before them: and his face did shine as the sun, and his raiment was white as the light.*

During Jesus' crucifixion, some of the onlookers wonder if Elijah would come to rescue him, as by the time of Jesus, Elijah was a legend as a rescuer of Jews in distress. The truth be known is that many of us have been killed many times throughout our lifetimes for our abilities.

Elijah makes an appearance in the New Testament during an incident known as the Transfiguration. At the summit of an unnamed mount, Jesus' face begins to shine. The disciples who are with Him hear the voice of God announce that Jesus is "My beloved Son."

The disciples also see Moses and Elijah appear and talk with Jesus. Peter is so struck by the experience that he asks Jesus if they should not build three "tabernacles"—one for Elijah, one for Jesus and one for Moses.

**Matthew 17 (KJV)**
*¹And after six days Jesus taketh Peter, James, and John his brother, and bringeth them up into an high mountain apart, ²And was transfigured before them: and his face did shine as the sun, and his raiment was white as the light. ³And, behold, there appeared unto them Moses and Elias talking with him. ⁴Then answered Peter, and said unto Jesus, Lord, it is good for us to be here: if thou wilt, let us make here three tabernacles; one for thee, and one for Moses, and one for Elias. ⁵While he yet spake, behold, a bright cloud overshadowed them: and behold a voice out of the cloud, which said, This is my beloved Son, in whom I am well pleased; hear ye him. ⁶And when the disciples heard it, they fell on their face, and were sore afraid. ⁷And Jesus came and touched them, and said, Arise, and be not afraid. ⁸And when they had lifted up their eyes, they saw no man, save Jesus only. ⁹And as they came down from the mountain, Jesus charged them, saying, Tell the vision to no man, until the Son of man be risen again from the dead. ¹⁰And his disciples asked him, saying, Why then say the scribes that Elias must first come? ¹¹And Jesus answered and said unto them, Elias truly shall first come, and restore all things. ¹²But I say unto you, That Elias is come already, and they knew him not, but have done unto him whatsoever they listed. Likewise shall also the Son of man suffer of them.*

## *MOSES COMES FIRST*

Moses comes first before Elijah and Moses came first at the time of Jesus when he incarnated as John the Baptist. The reason there is much confusion over the text referring to John the Baptist versus Elijah is because at the Transfiguration, Moses and Elijah both appear. Elijah is an aspect of Jesus and Moses is an aspect of John the Baptist. ☺

Moses/John the Baptist are also one of the three personalities that the Christ has given the power of his spirit.

**Luke 1:13-19 (KJV)**
*¹³But the angel said unto him, Fear not, Zacharias: for thy prayer is heard; and thy wife Elisabeth shall bear thee a son, and thou shalt call his name John. ¹⁴And thou shalt have joy and gladness; and many*

*shall rejoice at his birth. ¹⁵For he shall be great in the sight of the Lord, and shall drink neither wine nor strong drink; and he shall be filled with the Holy Ghost, even from his mother's womb. ¹⁶And many of the children of Israel shall he turn to the Lord their God.*

*¹⁷And he shall go before him in the spirit and power of Elias, to turn the hearts of the fathers to the children, and the disobedient to the wisdom of the just; to make ready a people prepared for the Lord. ¹⁸And Zacharias said unto the angel, whereby shall I know this? for I am an old man, and my wife well stricken in years. ¹⁹And the angel answering said unto him, I am Gabriel, that stand in the presence of God; and am sent to speak unto thee, and to shew thee these glad tidings.*

Jesus uses Elijah as an example of rejected prophets. Jesus says, "No prophet is accepted in his own country," and then mentions Elijah, saying that there were many widows in Israel, but Elijah was sent to one in Phoenicia. In Romans 11:1-6, Paul cites Elijah as an example of God's never forsaking his people (the Israelites).

**James 5:16-18 (KJV)**
*¹⁶Confess your faults one to another, and pray one for another, that ye may be healed. The effectual fervent prayer of a righteous man availeth much. ¹⁷Elias was a man subject to like passions as we are, and he prayed earnestly that it might not rain: and it rained not on the Earth by the space of three years and six months. ¹⁸And he prayed again, and the heaven gave rain, and the Earth brought forth her fruit.*

James says, "The effectual passionate prayer of a righteous man availeth much," and then cites Elijah's prayers that started and ended the famine in Israel as examples.

**Ecclesiasticus 48:10**

> "At the appointed time, it is written, you are destined
> to calm the wrath of God before it breaks out in fury,
> to turn the hearts of parents to their children,
> and to restore the tribes of Jacob."

Jonah, the widow's son, has also come again, waiting in spirit form (has left his physical body) on this side of the veil yet to cross over until he fulfills his purpose. When Jonah reincarnated into this time in history, he chose not to cross over into the light with the other spirits because he had very important unfinished business. Elijah saved Jonah in that life with the widow. Jonah is determined to repay his karmic commitment to Elijah before crossing over. Jonah can cross over anytime he wishes but has chosen to stay on this side of the veil, ensuring the safety of Elijah. Angels and ascended masters can transform or materialize to help a human being, but it requires an extended amount of energy to do so.

We are spirits having a human experience. We choose how we come and how we leave—we also choose when, how, where and why. It's a grand plan that involves everyone. We are never alone and we do not work alone. ☺

**1 Kings 17 (KJV)**
*[17]And it came to pass after these things, that the son of the woman, the mistress of the house, fell sick; and his sickness was so sore, that there was no breath left in him. [18]And she said unto Elijah, What have I to do with thee, O thou man of God? art thou come unto me to call my sin to remembrance, and to slay my son? [19]And he said unto her, Give me thy son. And he took him out of her bosom, and carried him up into a loft, where he abode, and laid him upon his own bed. [20]And he cried unto the LORD, and said, O LORD my God, hast thou also brought evil upon the widow with whom I sojourn, by slaying her son? [21]And he stretched himself upon the child three times, and cried unto the LORD, and said, O LORD my God, I pray thee, let this child's soul come into him again. [22]And the LORD heard the voice of Elijah; and the soul of the child came into him again, and he revived. [23]And Elijah took the child, and brought him down out of the chamber into the house, and delivered him unto his mother: and Elijah said, See, thy son liveth. [24]And the woman said to Elijah, Now by this I know that thou art a man of God, and that the word of the LORD in thy mouth is truth.*

This is not the first time Jonah left his physical body and stayed on this side of the veil in spirit form. Remember when Jonah was swallowed by the whale? Some souls do not cross over immediately after leaving their physical body for various reasons. They are free to cross anytime they wish. Their guides and angels never leave them.

## The Story of Jonah's Near Death Experience

Jonah son of Amittai appears in 2 Kings as a prophet from Gath-Hepher (a few miles north of Nazareth), active during the reign of Jeroboam II (c. 786-746 BC), where he predicts that Jeroboam will recover certain lost territories.

Jonah is also the central character in the Book of Jonah. Ordered by God to go to the city of Nineveh to prophesy against it "for their great wickedness is come up before me." Jonah seeks instead to flee from "the presence of the Lord" by going to Jaffa and sailing to Tarshish, which, geographically, is in the opposite direction. A huge storm arises and the sailors, realizing this is no ordinary storm, cast lots and learn that Jonah is to blame. Jonah admits this and states that if he is thrown overboard, the storm will cease.

The sailors try to dump as much cargo as possible before giving up, but feel forced to throw him overboard, at which point the sea calms. The inspired sailors then offer sacrifices to God. Jonah is miraculously saved (Jonah has a "Near Death Experience) by being swallowed by a large fish specially prepared by God in which he spent three days and three nights (reviewing his soul journey and what still needed to be accomplished by Jonah here on Earth).

In chapter two, while in the great fish, Jonah prays to God in his affliction and commits to thanksgiving and to paying what he has vowed. God commands the fish to vomit Jonah out so that he may complete his unfinished business. The first time Jonah prays in the book is in the fish, which is also the first time Jonah rejoices. In 1554, the French naturalist Guillaume Rondelet had carefully analyzed the anatomical aspects of the biblical story of Jonah and the fish. He concluded that the windpipe and lungs of a whale were so placed that it would be unlikely that it could swallow a man whole. God again orders Jonah to visit Nineveh and to prophesy to its inhabitants. This time he goes and enters the city crying, "In forty days Nineveh shall be overthrown." After Jonah walked for a day across Nineveh, the people of Nineveh began to believe his word and proclaimed a fast. The king of Nineveh puts on sackcloth and sits in ashes, making a proclamation to decree fasting, sackcloth, prayer and repentance. God sees their works and spares the city at that time. The entire city is humbled and broken with the people (and even the animals) in sackcloths and ashes. Animals, plants, warmth and even fish are all seen under the sovereign hand of God. Even the king comes off his throne to repent.

Displeased by this, Jonah refers to his earlier flight to Tarshish while asserting that, since God is merciful, it was inevitable that God would turn from the threatened calamities. He then leaves the city and makes himself a shelter, waiting to see whether or not the city will be destroyed.

God causes a plant (in Hebrew a Kikayon) to grow over Jonah's shelter to give him some shade from the sun. Later, God causes a worm to bite the plant's root and it withers. Jonah, now being exposed to the full force of the sun, becomes faint and desires that God take him out of the world.

And God said to Jonah, "Art thou greatly angry for the Kikayon?" And Jonah said, "I am greatly angry, even unto death." And the Lord said, "Thou hast had pity on the gourd, for which thou hast not laboured, neither madest it grow, which came up in a night, and perished in a night; and should not I have pity on Nineveh, that great city, wherein are more than sixscore thousand persons that cannot discern between their right hand and their left hand, and also much cattle?"—***Jonah, 4: 9-11***

Sometimes our lives are cut off short, before our time. Your age is not a factor in it *"being your time"*. My son, he was young in this life; he completed what he came here to do. It was his time to return home to the Creator so that he could continue with the plan we have all made together.

Jonah, however, incarnated in this time in history—it wasn't his time and he had some very important work to complete. Jonah chose to wait on this side in spirit form—this is quite a sacrifice.

However, during the soultime of his lifetime as Jonah he had two near death experiences, one as a young boy when Elijah brought his soul back into his body and a second time when he is thrown overboard into the water! After three days and three nights, his soul is returned as he agreed to help the son of man move forward on his spiritual path.

You have likely heard many stories of others who have had near death experiences—there are boatloads of stories out there of what people are saying happened to them while they were on the other side. One of the most compelling near death experiences that I am aware of happened to John Scott who explained to me how it changed his life 100% in every area of his thinking, action and speech. He told me he came back with knowledge that he couldn't possibly have known prior, especially in area of spiritual knowledge, earth's true history, particle physics, extra terrestrials and the structure of our cosmos from our DNA right up to the vastest big bang theory, which is ongoing!

His soul returned to his body after three days and three nights—so that he could continue with "unfinished business" and believe me, you will not want to miss this! You can learn more about his message to the world by visiting his Youtube channel. http://www.youtube.com/user/johnscottartist or go to his website and discover his incredible gift in artistry! http://www.johnscottartist.com

If it is your time, it is your time. If you have unfinished business you will come back and your life will never be the same! Thank you John for all you do to help others wake up out of their sleep.

**Matthew 12:40-45 (KJV)**
*⁴⁰For as Jonas was three days and three nights in the whale's belly; so shall the Son of man be three days and three nights in the heart of the earth.*

Curiosity certainly did kill the cat—but then the cat had nine lives. I was willing to take the chance that I would have more than lives than a cat. ☺

How many times was I killed due to my curiosity, I wondered. This may surprise some of you—it turns out I have been killed many times before and I wasn't even a cat!☺ Don't laugh—so were you! Oh yes, dear sweet you!

**Revelation 6:9-11 (KJV)**
*⁹And when he had opened the fifth seal, I saw under the altar the souls of them that were slain for the word of God, and for the testimony which they held: ¹⁰And they cried with a loud voice, saying, How long, O Lord, holy and true, dost thou not judge and avenge our blood on them that dwell on the earth? ¹¹And white robes were given unto every one of them; and it was said unto them, that they should rest yet for a little season, until their fellow servants also and their brethren, that should be killed as they were, should be fulfilled.*

I have remembered who I was in the lifetime previous to this one—AND THEN the entire ball of yarn was starting to unravel. ☺ The **"WHY"** on my path started to become clearer. Now I had a new question: WHY Elijah? My first thoughts were questions, of course—could "Elijah" be the name of my book and was I "Elijah" in another life? I wasn't getting that "knowing" feeling quite like I would have expected, yet I KNEW there was some strong senses of more information yet to come, information that would lead me to the TRUTH. The journey continued . . .

## It Is a "SOUL" Journey

I have found **"The Kingdom of Heaven within The Holy Book of The Great Invisible Spirit**☺ I am an "old soul" who has had **many** lifetimes. Each lifetime is like playing a new part in a play so that I can experience another lesson, good or bad. When I depart, the lessons are reviewed. When I incarnate into the next life, I will leave home and go out into the Universe to learn new lessons that I have created with other soul family, including many of you reading this book. It's not much different than what we all do when we leave our home on Earth to be all we can be.

When I come back from my spiritual home, it is a continuous story. It is a soul journey. We are spirits; spirits never die. We don't remember who we are and where we came from or how we got here—we know this leaving the spirit realm. No wonder we all have the same thing on our minds throughout our lifetimes: Who AM I? Where did I come from? AND HOW did I get here? These are the basic questions imprinted in our DNA.

That is why the sets of possibilities and probabilities are established in an effort to rattle your memory enough to complete your life experiences with the same personality and the same light quotient. Each time you incarnate, you have new lessons and maybe some carried over from the previous life.

During each lifetime, we will increase our light through the lessons that we have come to experience. Did you know we carry over our personality into each life form? We use less than 10% of our total personality in each new incarnation onto this planet. It is our soul that carries our total personality. Our personality is our unique blueprint and is always with us. It is coded with all of our experiences throughout our soul's journey. The full use of the "blueprint" has been closed until the end of times. I have explained in much more detail in another chapter—you are going to love this!

Times are changing—the Galaxy, the Universe, the Earth and humanity are all evolving. We are living on the "New Earth" and we also need to evolve and match the vibration of this "New Earth". It is a Cosmic Event; everyone has been waiting for this throughout the Galaxy.☺ The frequencies are now available that have not been available until now. This is a historical event, the first time a spiritual being having a human experience doesn't have to leave the physical body to have paradise or "Heaven on Earth".

There is only one way home—through "The Holy Book" of the Great Invisible Spirit. If your **heart** so desires, you will have a spiritual transformation. The Great Invisible Spirit—your blueprint—is merely covered by a veil.

# PART III

# Treasures in the Kingdom of Heaven

**Matthew 6:19-21**

[19]Lay not up for yourselves treasures upon earth, where moth and rust doth corrupt, and where thieves break through and steal: [20]But lay up for yourselves treasures in heaven, where neither moth nor rust doth corrupt, and where thieves do not break through nor steal: [21]For where your treasure is, there will your heart be also.

## Chapter 9

# KNOWING ELIJAH

The ability of clairsentient, the gift of knowing, is one of the abilities that I have carried within my personality, part of my DNA blueprint from one lifetime to another. During my awakening, my rebirth into the fifth-dimensional energies, the awareness became known. It was part of the divine plan so that I could now write this book about past lives, reincarnation and the DNA at this exact time in history.

My ability to heal myself and others has always been carried with me. In some lifetimes, I was killed just like Jesus and John the Baptist were killed for their abilities. Some people thought because I could heal others and know things that I was a witch. In fact, the same people who received healings from me during that cycle were the same people who reported me and then had me killed. Thanks a bunch! But, I forgive you, and I hope you can forgive me, too.

The battle is not with each other, the battle is within. Imagine you are standing on the bank of the river and everything you need is on the other side. There are obstacles that you will need to overcome before you can even think about building a boat or going in for the big swim!

We all have past life experiences that are so painful and so sorrowful; we have blocked the knowledge of them which is holding you back from your truth. You must become a clear vessel with a pure heart. What you have done to others has also been done to you. It is time for forgiveness and for healing. The days of karma are over for those who chose the spiritual transformation.

**Matthew 7:12 (KJV)**
*[12] Therefore all things whatsoever ye would that men should do to you, do ye even so to them: for this is the law and the prophets.*

In another lifetime, I knew better and kept my knowing abilities to myself. In this particular lifetime, I was a widow and I wagered everything I had, which was one small meal left to feed my son and I. A stranger came and asked me to feed him. I explained that the food that I still had would be the last meal my son and I would eat. Then he said if I fed him, the food supply would be replenished every day. I knew Elijah was coming to make all things right.

## *HAPPY BIRTHDAY ELIJAH*

Elijah has come again to be here for this momentous Cosmic Event!

**2 Corinthians 13(KJV)**
*[1]This is the third time I am coming to you. In the mouth of two or three witnesses shall every word be established. [2]I told you before, and foretell you, as if I were present, the second time; and being absent now I write to them which heretofore have sinned, and to all other, that, if I come again, I will not spare:* This is the third time I am coming to you. Out of the mouth of two or three witnesses every word shall be recognized.

**Mark 9:9-13 (KJV)**
*[9]And as they came down from the mountain, he charged them that they should tell no man what things they had seen, till the Son of man were risen from the dead.* (As they came down from the mountain, Jesus told them that they should not tell anyone what they had seen till the son of man has awakened out of their sleep (mass awakening)).

*[10]And they kept that saying with themselves, questioning one with another what the rising from the dead should mean.* (rising from the dead means awakening out of a sleep)

*¹¹And they asked him, saying, Why say the scribes that Elias must first come?* (They asked why do the scribes (one who writes) say that Elijah must come first?)

*¹²And he answered and told them, Elias verily cometh first, and restoreth all things; and how it is written of the Son of man, that he must suffer many things, and be set at nought.* (He answered them and said Elijah happily comes first and restores all things. It has been written that the Son of man must suffer many things and set to nothing—have nothing left.) In other words, when man is at his lowest point—after having suffered from many things then Elijah will come.

*¹³But I say unto you, That Elias is indeed come, and they have done unto him whatsoever they listed, as it is written of him.* (I tell you, Elijah has come but they did not recognize him and they did to him whatever they wanted as it is written about him—in other words, the written word about Elijah is true but not written down as it being Elijah).

Jesus was talking about himself—as Elijah 800 years before. Both Jesus and John the Baptist suffered terrible deaths. Everyone assumed he was talking about John the Baptist because most people were not thinking or believing about reincarnation or past lives.

"ELIJAH" has already come and they did not recognize him. "ELIJAH" returned (reincarnated) into another physical body named "JESUS".

This information could not be told until now as requested by the Messiah. It was predestined to be told now at this momentous time on Earth—the New Earth. It could not be told because "son of man" was not ready until now. Mankind had to learn lessons of pain and suffering before he could understand joy and love. This was the only way the son of man could find the Kingdom of Heaven within the Holy Book of The Great Invisible Spirit☺.

## *The Mass Awakening—A Spiritual Transformation*

We are the ones we are waiting for—we have all been here many times before. Many souls are waiting to reincarnate right now to live in the physical on the "New Earth". You are the chosen ones to be here right now during this historical event!

Your lives played out during major historical events—and this time in history we have returned with many of our soul families to be a part of an event that we have all been waiting for for a very, very long time.

"ELIJAH/JESUS" has also come again to make things right. It is time to get ready, time to wake up out of your sleep. Elijah will bring together the hearts of fathers to their children and the hearts of the children to fathers. Elijah is the prophet/messiah in the Bible who does not die because none of us die—we are all spiritual beings having a human experience. He ascends into heaven on a chariot of fire, destined to witness the Kingdom of Heaven within the Holy Book of the Great Invisible Spirit☺. Elijah will witness man's entrance into the covenant of the Israelites (Elijah will witness man's entrance into the Holy Book of the Kingdom of Heaven). Elijah was multiplying food and bringing the dead to life some 800 years before his life as Jesus.

*Matthew 12:39-41 (KJV)*
*[39]But he answered and said unto them, an evil and adulterous generation seeketh after a sign; and there shall no sign be given to it, but the sign of the prophet Jonas: [40]For as Jonas was three days and three nights in the whale's belly; so shall the Son of man be three days and three nights in the heart of the earth. [41]The men of Nineveh shall rise in judgment with this generation, and shall condemn it: because they repented at the preaching of Jonas; and, behold, a greater than Jonas is here.* (Jonas/Jonah—A greater Jonas means he has reincarnated and is even better than the one who was here many times before.)

Each time we leave our physical body, the spirit transcends. The soul undergoes a process of awareness, acceptance and transformation—a dark night of the soul. After the spiritual transformation, the spirit will review his life from a much higher perspective. ☺

## *The Christ Consciousness*

The human mind has spiritual currents, vibrations of energy running through its thought streams. These vibrating streams contain vital information from *"SPIRIT"*—light and information that is ready for each soul who finds the Holy Book and prepares his house to bring Jacob home. Spirit is the source of everything TRUE, BEAUTIFUL and GOOD, and conveys these ideals through the human mind that interconnects with a person's beliefs, helping the individual ascend into the higher order that uplifts and improves the quality of life.

In human life, spiritual growth is achieved by aligning with these spiritual currents that come from both the personality and mind of Spirit by intellectual consent and emotional devotion. Christ Consciousness is the growing human acceptance and joining together of the human evolutionary mind with the divine mind and the divine personality that is the source of human happiness and fulfillment. This awareness increases throughout the lifetimes of the spiritual being. Knowing when intention, attention and openness is focused, one will come into that *"CHRISTED"* state of being—a state of enlightenment.

As this awareness in the human mind grows and strengthens, life becomes more free thinking, joyful, peaceful and love engaged. The fear that creates separation and despair begins to weaken in thought and feeling. You are free to live the life you were born to live as a child of Spirit in a love-filled and supportive Universe. The new energy, on the new Earth, brought this new message to tell you—a new door has opened in the Universe, allowing "olive" us the ability to live in the Kingdom of Heaven on Earth without having to leave your physical body.

*Chapter 11*

# BETTER THAN THE TIME BEFORE

### *The Age of Aquarius—The Golden Age*

***"The End Of The World As We Know It"***—this is the time for the end of old belief and systems that do not serve us anymore. Just the same as the world is ending as we know it, when you leave your physical body at the time of "death", it is not the end of your life—it is the end of your life as you know it. However, in this New Age, we no longer have to leave our tent (physical body) to have heaven or paradise on Earth.

It is a rebirth of the New Earth; the Earth has *reincarnated* into a New Dimension, the fifth dimension, with a higher vibration and a new energy—"Heaven on Earth". Get on your path to discover the spiritual being you are; go **within "The Holy Book of The Great Invisible Spirit".**

A spiritual transformation is required to ascend into the fifth-dimensional energies, a spiritual transformation to "the Kingdom of Heaven within the Holy Book of The Great Invisible Spirit ☺." It is a new beginning, a new place to create your dreams to your heart's content.

For some, it will be easy. For others, it may be more difficult. There are many light workers and world servers here to hold the door open for anyone willing to make the journey. ☺

There are many light workers and healers who are available in every corner of the planet, in every country and in every community to help you make the transition. Many have been appointed and positioned, available to assist the masses who are awakening out of their sleep. For more information, see www.sanetha.com.

**Daniel 12:4** But thou, O Daniel, shut up the words, and seal the book, even to the time of the end: many shall run to and fro, and knowledge shall be increased.

## *The Earth Reincarnated*

***Revelation 21*** *[1]And I saw a new heaven and a new earth: for the first heaven and the first earth were passed away; and there was no more sea.*

***Matthew 6:10*** *... Thy kingdom come, Thy will be done in earth, as it is in heaven.*

***Ecclesiastes 3:2*** *... a time to be born and a time to die, a time to plant and a time to uproot ...*

***Ecclesiastes 12:7*** *Then shall the dust return to the earth as it was: and the spirit shall return unto God who gave it.*

***Hebrews 13:8*** *Jesus Christ is the same yesterday, today, and forever.*

***Genesis 2:3-5*** *[3]And God blessed the seventh day, and sanctified it: because that in it he had rested from all his work which God created and made. [4]These are the generations of the heavens and of the earth when they were created, in the day that the LORD God made the earth and the heavens, [5]And every plant of the field before it was in the earth, and every herb of the field before it grew: for the LORD God had not caused it to rain upon the earth, and there was not a man to till the ground*

Following Jesus' ministry, reincarnation and the path of personal Christhood was taught for several hundred years by Christian Gnostics, until their ministry was shut down by church hierarchy for human power and political gain.

## EVOLUTION

### *Each Time We Incarnate, We Return Better Than The Time Before*

**Luke 13:32**
*32 And he said unto them, Go ye, and tell that fox, Behold, I cast out devils, and I do cures today and tomorrow, and the third day I shall be perfected.*

And he said to them, Go you, and tell that sly fox, I will do my work casting out demons today, tomorrow, and the third day will be perfected. In other words, with each incarnation he brings with him in his personality healing abilities that will be better than the time before.

*Chapter 999*

# MOTHER, FATHER, GOD

As the "Christ Consciousness" comes to light, son of man will discover a field of dreams comes together from years of despair and separation, and is available in ways never before imagined possible. The gifts and abilities you possess become unplugged within your own land, your own temple, your own house, your physical body (tent). There is no amount of money that can buy or take away from those who find the "Holy Book".

## *THE TWINS*

**Genesis 25:21-27 (KJV)**
[21] And Isaac intreated the LORD for his wife, because she was barren: and the LORD was intreated of him, and Rebekah his wife conceived. [22] And the children struggled together within her; and she said, If it be so, why am I thus? And she went to enquire of the LORD. [23] And the LORD said unto her, **Two nations are in thy womb, and two manner of people shall be separated** from thy bowels; and the one people shall be stronger than the other people; and the elder shall serve the younger. [24] And when her days to be delivered were fulfilled, behold, there were twins in her womb. [25] **And the first came out red, all over like an hairy garment; and they called his name Esau.** [26] And after that came his brother out, and his hand took hold on Esau's heel; and his name was called Jacob: and Isaac was threescore years old when she bare them. [27] And the boys grew: and Esau was a cunning hunter, a man of the field; and Jacob was a plain man, dwelling in tents.

## *Jacob's Homecoming*

Jacob was separated from his family and homeland in search of the "Promised Land"—a term used to describe the land promised or given by God to the Israelites, the descendants of Jacob.

**Genesis 28:11-17 (KJV)**
*[11]And he lighted upon a certain place, and tarried there all night, because the sun was set; and he took of the stones of that place, and put them for his pillows, and lay down in that place to sleep. [12]And he dreamed, and behold a ladder set up on the earth, and the top of it reached to heaven: and behold the angels of God ascending and descending on it.*

*[13]And, behold, the LORD stood above it, and said, I am the LORD God of Abraham thy father, and the God of Isaac: the land whereon thou liest, to thee will I give it, and to thy seed; [14]And thy seed shall be as the dust of the earth, and thou shalt spread abroad to the west, and to the east, and to the north, and to the south: and in thee and in thy seed shall all the families of the earth be blessed.*

*[15]And, behold, I am with thee, and will keep thee in all places whither thou goest, and will bring thee again into this land; for I will not leave thee, until I have done that which I have spoken to thee of. [16]And Jacob awaked out of his sleep, and he said, Surely the LORD is in this place; and I knew it not. [17]And he was afraid, and said, How dreadful is this place! this is none other but the house of God, and this is the gate of heaven.*

**Isaiah 49:5-7 (KJV)**
*[5]And now, saith the LORD that formed me from the womb to be his servant, to **bring Jacob again to him**, Though Israel be not gathered, yet shall I be glorious in the eyes of the LORD, and my God shall be my strength.*

*[6]And he said, It is a light thing that thou shouldest be my servant to **raise up the tribes of Jacob**, and to restore the preserved of Israel: I*

*will also give thee for a light to the Gentiles, that thou mayest be my salvation unto the end of the earth.*

*⁷**Thus saith the LORD, the Redeemer of Israel, and his Holy One**, to him whom man despiseth, to him whom the nation abhorreth, to a servant of rulers, Kings shall see and arise, princes also shall worship, because of the LORD that is faithful, and the Holy One of Israel, and he shall choose thee.*

## ISRAEL

Israel: The ancient kingdom of the 12 Hebrew tribes at the SE end of the Mediterranean

Israel: **IS**—Female/Mother; **RA**—Male/Father ; **EL**—God

**Mother/Father/God**

**I·SIS** *in mythology*—An ancient Egyptian goddess of fertility, the sister and wife of Osiris

**RA,** also **RE** *in mythology*—The ancient Egyptian sun god, the supreme deity represented as a man with the head of a hawk crowned with a solar disk and uraeus

**EL**—Name for God meaning strength, might or power; the true God of IsRaEl

## Jacob

In the Old Testament, Jacob (later called Israel) is the son of Isaac and Rebekah and the father of the 12 founders of the 12 tribes of Israel. He was born holding his twin brother Esau's heel, and his name is explained as meaning "holder of the heel" or to take the place or position of somebody by force or maneuver.

**Jacob** ("heel" or "leg-puller") also later known as **Israel** ("persevere with God") was the third patriarch of the Hebrew people with whom God made a covenant and ancestor of the tribes of Israel, which were named after his descendants.

He is the son of Isaac and Rebekah, the grandson of Abraham and Sarah and of Bethuel, and the younger twin brother of Esau. He had 12 sons and at least one daughter by his two wives, Leah and Rachel, and by their female slaves, Bilhah and Zilpah. The children named in Genesis were Reuben, Simeon, Levi, Judah, Dan, Naphtali, Gad, Asher, Issachar, Zebulun, daughter Dinah, Joseph and Benjamin.

Before the birth of Benjamin, Jacob is renamed "Israel" by an angel. The name "Israel" can be translated as "God contended", but other meanings have also been suggested. Some commentators say the name comes from the verb *śœarar* ("to rule, be strong, have authority over"), thereby making the name mean "God rules" or "God judges". Other possible meanings include "the prince of God" (from the King James version) or "El fights/struggles".

The King James version is the authorized version, commonly known as the *King James Version*, *King James Bible* or *KJV*, and is an English translation of the Christian Bible by the Church of England begun in 1604 and completed in 1611.

As a result of a severe drought in Canaan, Jacob moved to Egypt at the time when his son Joseph was viceroy. Jacob died there 17 years later, and Joseph carried Jacob's remains to the land of Canaan, where he gave them stately burial in the same Cave of Machpelah as were buried Abraham, Sarah, Isaac, Rebekah and Jacob's wife, Leah.

## *Jacob and Esau's Birth*

Jacob and his twin brother, Esau, were born to Isaac and Rebekah after 20 years of marriage, when Isaac was 60 (Genesis 25:20, 25:26).

Rebekah was uncomfortable during her double pregnancy and went to inquire of God why she was suffering. She received the prophecy that the twins were fighting in her womb and would continue to fight all their lives, even after they became two separate nations. The prophecy also said that the older would serve the younger; from it, the statement "one people will be stronger than the other" has been taken to mean that the two nations would never gain power simultaneously; when one fell, the other would rise and vice versa. According to traditional accounts, Rebekah did not share the prophecy with her husband.

When the time came for Rebekah to give birth, the first to come out emerged red and hairy all over, with his heel grasped by the hand of the second to come out. According to Genesis 25:25, Isaac and Rebekah named the first Esau (Esav or Esaw, meaning "hairy" or "rough", "do" or "make"; or "completely developed"). The second was named Jacob, meaning "heel-catcher", "supplanter", "leg-puller", "he who follows upon the heels of one", "seize by the heel", "circumvent" or "restrain".

The boys displayed very different natures as they matured. ". . . and Esau was a cunning hunter, a man of the field; but Jacob was a simple man, dwelling in tents . . ." Moreover, the attitudes of their parents toward them also differed, "And Isaac loved Esau because he did eat of his venison: but Rebekah loved Jacob."

"The boys displayed very different natures as they matured . . . and Esau was a cunning hunter, a man of the field." **Esau was a man of the field—a spiritual man living in the Kingdom of Heaven.**

". . . but Jacob was a simple man, dwelling in tents." **Jacob was dwelling in the physical body separated and out of touch or lost from his spiritual body.**

**Note:** Tents are what is meant upon our incarnating into a physical body and the field is where spirits reside.

## Sale of the birthright—represents the separation of our God-given birthrights

The Hebrew Bible in Genesis 25:29-34 tells the account of Esau selling his birthright to Jacob. This passage states that Esau, returning hungry from the fields, begged Jacob to give him some of the stew that Jacob had just made. (Esau referred to the dish as, "that same red pottage", giving rise to his nickname☺ *Edom*, meaning "Red".) Jacob offered to give Esau a bowl of stew in exchange for his birthright.

**Genesis 25:29-34 (KJV)**
*[29]And Jacob sod pottage: and Esau came from the field, and he was faint: [30]And Esau said to Jacob, Feed me, I pray thee, with that same red pottage; for I am faint: therefore was his name called Edom. [31]And Jacob said, Sell me this day thy birthright. [32]And Esau said, Behold, I am at the point to die: and what profit shall this birthright do to me? [33]And Jacob said, Swear to me this day; and he sware unto him: and he sold his birthright unto Jacob. [34]Then Jacob gave Esau bread and pottage of lentiles; and he did eat and drink, and rose up, and went his way: thus Esau despised his birthright and agreed.*

According to Wikipedia, Esau, a "son of the desert" became a hunter who had "rough qualities that distinguished him from his twin brother". Jacob was a shy or simple man, depending on the translation of the Hebrew word "Tam" (which also means "relatively perfect man". Throughout Genesis, Esau is frequently shown as being supplanted by his younger twin, Jacob (Israel)

**Jacob's Deception of Isaac**
As Isaac aged, he became blind and was uncertain when he would die, so he decided to bestow Esau's birthright upon him. He requested that Esau go out to the fields with his weapons (quiver and bow) to kill some venison. Isaac went on to request that Esau make "savory meat" for him out of the venison, according to the way he enjoyed it the most, so that he could eat it and bless Esau.

Rebekah overheard this conversation. It is suggested that she realized prophetically that Isaac's blessings would go to Jacob, since she was told before the twins' birth that the older son would serve the younger. She quickly ordered Jacob to bring her two kid goats from their flock so that he could take Esau's place in serving Isaac and receiving his blessing. Jacob protested that his father would recognize their deception, since Esau was hairy and he himself was smooth-skinned. He feared his father would curse him as soon as he felt him, but Rebekah offered to take the curse herself, then insisted that Jacob obey her. Jacob did as his mother instructed and when he returned with the kids, Rebekah made the savory meat that Isaac loved. Before she sent Jacob to his father, she dressed him in Esau's garments and laid goatskins on his arms and neck to simulate hairy skin.

Disguised as Esau, Jacob entered Isaac's room. Surprised that Esau was supposedly back so soon, Isaac asked how it could be that the hunt went so quickly. Jacob responded, "Because the Lord your God brought it to me." Rashi in Genesis 27:21 says Isaac's suspicions were aroused even more, because Esau never used the personal name of God. Isaac demanded that Jacob come close so he could feel him, but the goatskins felt just like Esau's hairy skin. Confused, Isaac exclaimed, "The voice is Jacob's voice, but the hands are the hands of Esau!" (Genesis 27:22).

Still trying to get at the truth, Isaac asked him directly, "Art thou my very son Esau?" and Jacob answered simply, "I am." Isaac proceeded to eat the food and to drink the wine that Jacob gave him, and then told him to come close and kiss him. As Jacob kissed his father, Isaac smelled the clothes which belonged to Esau and finally accepted that the person in front of him was Esau. Isaac then blessed Jacob with the blessing that was meant for Esau. **Genesis 27:28-29** states Isaac's blessing: "Therefore God give thee of the dew of heavens, and the fatness of the earth, and plenty of corn and wine: Let people serve thee: be lord over thy brethren, and let thy mother's sons bow down to thee: cursed be every one that curseth thee, and blessed be he that blesseth thee."

Jacob had scarcely left the room when Esau returned from the hunt to prepare his game and receive the blessing. The realization that he had been deceived shocked Isaac, yet he acknowledged that Jacob had received the blessings by adding, "Indeed, he will be [or remain] blessed!" (Genesis 27:33).

Esau was *heartbroken* by the deception and begged for his own blessing. Having made Jacob a ruler over his brothers, Isaac could only promise, "By your sword you shall live, but your brother you shall serve; yet it shall be that when you are aggrieved, you may cast off his yoke from upon your neck" (Genesis 27:39-40).

Esau was filled with hatred toward Jacob for taking away both his birthright and his blessing. He vowed to himself to kill Jacob as soon as Isaac died. When Rebekah heard about his murderous intentions, she ordered Jacob to travel to her brother Laban's house in Haran until Esau's anger subsided. She convinced Isaac to send Jacob away by telling him that she despaired of him marrying a local girl from the idol-worshipping families of Canaan (as Esau had done). After Isaac sent Jacob away to find a wife, Esau realized his own Canaanite wives were evil in his father's eyes, and he took a daughter of Isaac's half-brother Ishmael as another wife.

# Chapter IV

# SIGNS OF THE TIMES

*Stairway to Heaven*

And as we wind on down the road
Our shadows taller than our soul.
There walks a lady we all know
Who shines white light and wants to show
How everything still turns to gold.
And if you listen very hard
The tune will come to you at last.
When all are one and one is all
To be a rock and not to roll.
And she's buying the stairway to heaven.

**—Led Zeppelin**

## *Jacob's Ladder*

**Jacob's Ladder, early 1900s Bible illustration**

Nearby Luz en route to Haran, Jacob experienced a vision of a ladder or staircase reaching into heaven with angels going up and down it, commonly referred to as "Jacob's Ladder". From the top of the ladder he heard the voice of God, who repeated many of the blessings upon him.

According to Rashi, this ladder signified the exiles that the Jewish people would suffer before the coming of the Jewish Messiah. The angels that represented the exiles of Babylonia, Persia and Greece each climbed up a certain number of steps, paralleling the years of the exile, before they "fell down", but the angel representing the last exile, that of Rome or Edom, kept climbing higher and higher into the clouds. Jacob feared that his children would never be free of Esau's domination, but God assured him that at the **End of Days**, Edom too would come falling down.

Jacob awakened and continued on his way to Haran in the morning, naming the place "Bethel", or "God's house".

Arriving in Haran, Jacob saw a well where the shepherds were gathering their flocks to water them and met Laban's younger daughter, Rachel, Jacob's first cousin; she was working as a shepherdess. He loved her immediately, and after spending a month with his relatives, asked for her hand in marriage in return for working seven years for Laban. Laban agreed to the arrangement. These seven years seemed to Jacob "but a few days, for the love he had for her"; but when they were complete and he asked for his wife, Laban deceived Jacob by switching Rachel's older sister, Leah, as the veiled bride.

**Rachel and Jacob by William Dyce**

In the morning, when the truth became known, Laban justified himself, saying that in his country it was unheard of to give the younger daughter before the older. However, he agreed to give Rachel in marriage as well if Jacob would work another seven years for her. After the week of wedding celebrations with Leah, Jacob married Rachel and he continued to work for Laban for another seven years.

Jacob loved Rachel more than Leah, and Leah felt hated. God opened Leah's womb and she gave birth to four sons rapidly: Reuben, Simeon, Levi and Judah. Rachel, however, remained barren. Following the example of Sarah, who gave her handmaid to Abraham after years of infertility, Rachel gave Jacob her handmaid, Bilhah, in marriage, so that Rachel could raise children through her. Bilhah gave birth to Dan and Naphtali. Seeing that she had left off childbearing temporarily, Leah then gave her handmaid Zilpah to Jacob in marriage so that Leah could raise more children through her. Zilpah gave birth to Gad and Asher. (According to The Testaments of the Patriarchs, Bilhah and Zilpah were the daughters of Rotheus and Euna, servants of Laban.) Afterwards, Leah became fertile again and gave birth to Issachar, Zebulun and Dinah. God remembered Rachel, who gave birth to Joseph. If pregnancies of different marriages overlapped, the

12 births could have occurred within seven years (the first 11 births occurred within six years, according to Genesis 31:38).

After Joseph was born, Jacob decided to return home to his parents. Laban was reluctant to release him, as God had blessed his flock on account of Jacob. Laban asked what he could pay Jacob, and Jacob proposed that all the spotted, speckled and brown goats and sheep of Laban's flock, at any given moment, would be his wages. Jacob placed peeled rods of poplar, hazel, and chestnut within the flocks' watering holes or troughs, an action he later attributed to a dream. The text suggests that Jacob performed breeding experiments over the years to make his own flocks both more abundant and stronger than Laban's, and that Laban responded by repeatedly reinterpreting the terms of Jacob's wages, and that the breeding favored Jacob regardless of Laban's pronouncements. Thus Jacob's herds increased and he became very wealthy.

As time passed, Laban's sons noticed that Jacob was taking the better part of their flocks, and Laban's friendly attitude towards Jacob began to change. God told Jacob that he should leave, and he and his wives and children did so without informing Laban. Before they left, Rachel stole the teraphim, considered to be household idols, from Laban's house.

In a rage, Laban pursued Jacob for seven days. The night before he caught up to him, God appeared to Laban in a dream and warned him not to say anything good or bad to Jacob. When the two met, Laban played the part of the injured father-in-law and also demanded his *teraphim* back. Knowing nothing about Rachel's theft, Jacob told Laban that whoever stole them should die, and stood aside to let him search. When Laban reached Rachel's tent, she hid the *teraphim* by sitting on them and stating she could not get up because she was menstruating; this event was considered by the biblical audience as significant defilement upon the *teraphim*. Jacob and Laban then parted from each other with a pact to preserve the peace between them. Laban returned to his home and Jacob continued on his way.

## *Jacob's Inner Struggle*

**Jacob struggles with the angel, by Rembrandt**

**Genesis 32:24 (KJV)**
*²⁴And Jacob was left alone; and there wrestled a man with him until the breaking of the day.*

As Jacob neared the land of Canaan, he sent messengers ahead to his brother Esau. They returned with the news that Esau was coming to meet Jacob with an army of 400 men. With great apprehension, Jacob prepared for the worst. He engaged in earnest prayer to God, then sent on before him a tribute of flocks and herds to Esau, "a present to my lord Esau from thy servant Jacob".

Jacob then transported his family and flocks across the ford Jabbok by night, then recrossed back to send over his possessions, being left alone in communion with God. There, a mysterious being appeared and the two wrestled until daybreak.

Jacob then demanded a blessing and the being declared that from then on, Jacob would be called Israel (*Yisra'el*, meaning "one that struggled with the divine angel").

Afterwards, Jacob named the place Penuel (*Penuw`el*, *Peniy`el*, meaning "face of God"), saying, "I have seen God face to face and lived."

*(René Descartes (1596-1650) maintained that the pineal gland is the part of the body with which the soul is most immediately associated.)*

In the morning, Jacob assembled his four wives and 11 sons, placing the maidservants and their children in front, Leah and her children next, and Rachel and Joseph in the rear. Some commentators cite this placement as proof that Jacob continued to favor Joseph over Leah's children, as presumably the rear position would have been safer from a frontal assault by Esau, which Jacob feared. Jacob himself took the foremost position. Esau's spirit of revenge, however, was apparently appeased by Jacob's bounteous gifts of camels, goats and flocks. Their reunion was an emotional one.

Esau offered to accompany them on their way back to Israel, but Jacob protested that his children were still young and tender (born 6 to 13 years prior in the narrative), so Jacob suggested eventually catching up with Esau at Mount Seir. According to the Sages, this was a prophetic reference to the End of Days, when Jacob's descendants will come to Mount Seir, the home of Edom, to deliver judgment against Esau's descendants for persecuting them throughout the millennia (see Obadiah 1:21). Jacob actually diverted himself to Succoth and was not recorded as rejoining Esau until, at Machpelah, the two bury their father Isaac, who lived to 180 and was 60 years older than them.

Jacob then arrived in Shechem, where he bought a parcel of land, now identified as Joseph's Tomb.

Jacob then made a further move while Rachel was pregnant; near Bethlehem, Rachel went into labor and died as she gave birth to her second son, Benjamin (Jacob's 12th son). Jacob buried her and erected a monument over her grave.

When Isaac died at the age of 180, Jacob and Esau buried him in the Cave of the Patriarchs, which Abraham had purchased as a family burial plot.

## *The Coat of Many Colours*

Jacob's 11th son, Joseph, after receiving a coat of many colors had many dreams.

**Genesis 37:5-9 (KJV)**
*⁵And Joseph dreamed a dream, and he told it his brethren: and they hated him yet the more. ⁶And he said unto them, Hear, I pray you, this dream which I have dreamed: ⁷For, behold, we were binding sheaves in the field, and, lo, my sheaf arose, and also stood upright; and, behold, your sheaves stood round about, and made obeisance to my sheaf. ⁸And his brethren said to him, Shalt thou indeed reign over us? or shalt thou indeed have dominion over us? And they hated him yet the more for his dreams, and for his words. ⁹And he dreamed yet another dream, and told it his brethren, and said, Behold, I have dreamed a dream more; and, behold, the sun and the moon and the eleven stars made obeisance to me.*

## Joseph The Dreamer

The house of Jacob dwelt in Hebron, in the land of Canaan. His flocks were often fed in the pastures of Shechem as well as Dothan. Of all the children in his household, he loved Rachel's firstborn son, Joseph, the most. Thus Joseph's half brothers were jealous of him and they ridiculed him often. Joseph even told his father about all of his half brothers' misdeeds. When Joseph was 17 years old, Jacob made a long coat or tunic of many colors for him. Seeing this, the half brothers began to hate Joseph. Then Joseph began to have dreams that implied that his family would bow down to him. When he told his brothers about these dreams, it drove them to conspire against him. When Jacob heard of these dreams, he criticized his son for proposing the idea that the house of Jacob would even bow down to Joseph. Yet, he contemplated his son's words about these dreams.

The coat was symbolic, meaning Joseph had many lifetimes (many "colors"). Joseph had gifts and abilities that not only did he bring with him in this lifetime, but he chose to have the ability available in order to create the experiences for that lifetime, which included bringing the message needed at that time in history.

## Joseph's Coat Brought to Jacob

Wikipedia goes into more detail stating sometime afterward, the sons of Jacob by Leah, Bilhah and Zilpah were feeding his flocks in Shechem. Jacob wanted to know how things were doing, so he asked Joseph to go down there and return with a report. This was the last time he would ever see his son in Hebron. Later that day, the report that Jacob ended up receiving came from Joseph's brothers who brought before him a coat laden with blood. Jacob identified the coat as the one he made for Joseph. At that moment, he cried, "It is my son's tunic. A wild beast has devoured him. Without doubt Joseph is torn to pieces." He rid his clothes and put a sackcloth around his waist in mourning for days. No one from the house of Jacob could comfort him during this time of bereavement (Genesis 37:31-35).

The truth was Jacob's son Joseph was turned in by his brothers and ultimately sold into slavery on a caravan headed for Egypt (Genesis 37:36).

Joseph was separated from his family, separated from the sons of Jacob—hidden as his father was not aware that he was alive.

## Coming to Terms

### Genesis 32 (KJV)
*¹And Jacob went on his way, and the angels of God met him. ²And when Jacob saw them, he said, this is God's host: and he called the name of that place Mahanaim. ³And Jacob sent messengers before him to Esau his brother unto the land of Seir, the country of Edom. ⁴And he commanded them, saying, Thus shall ye speak unto my lord Esau; Thy servant Jacob saith thus, I have sojourned with Laban, and stayed there until now: ⁵And I have oxen, and asses, flocks, and menservants, and women servants: and I have sent to tell my lord, that I may find*

*grace in thy sight.* ⁶*And the messengers returned to Jacob, saying, We came to thy brother Esau, and also he cometh to meet thee, and four hundred men with him.* ⁷*Then Jacob was greatly afraid and distressed: and he divided the people that was with him, and the flocks, and herds, and the camels, into two bands;* ⁸*And said, If Esau come to the one company, and smite it, then the other company which is left shall escape.* ⁹*And Jacob said, O God of my father Abraham, and God of my father Isaac, the LORD which saidst unto me, Return unto thy country, and to thy kindred, and I will deal well with thee:* ¹⁰*I am not worthy of the least of all the mercies, and of all the truth, which thou hast shewed unto thy servant; for with my staff I passed over this Jordan; and now I am become two bands.* ¹¹*Deliver me, I pray thee, from the hand of my brother, from the hand of Esau: for I fear him, lest he will come and smite me, and the mother with the children.* ¹²*And thou saidst, I will surely do thee good, and make thy seed as the sand of the sea, which cannot be numbered for multitude.* ¹³*And he lodged there that same night; and took of that which came to his hand a present for Esau his brother;* ¹⁴*Two hundred she goats, and twenty he goats, two hundred ewes, and twenty rams,* ¹⁵*Thirty milch camels with their colts, forty kine, and ten bulls, twenty she asses, and ten foals.* ¹⁶*And he delivered them into the hand of his servants, every drove by themselves; and said unto his servants, Pass over before me, and put a space betwixt drove and drove.* ¹⁷*And he commanded the foremost, saying, When Esau my brother meeteth thee, and asketh thee, saying, Whose art thou? and whither goest thou? and whose are these before thee?* ¹⁸*Then thou shalt say, They be thy servant Jacob's; it is a present sent unto my lord Esau: and, behold, also he is behind us.* ¹⁹*And so commanded he the second, and the third, and all that followed the droves, saying, On this manner shall ye speak unto Esau, when ye find him.* ²⁰*And say ye moreover, Behold, thy servant Jacob is behind us. For he said, I will appease him with the present that goeth before me, and afterward I will see his face; peradventure he will accept of me.* ²¹*So went the present over before him: and himself lodged that night in the company.* ²²*And he rose up that night, and took his two wives, and his two women servants, and his eleven sons, and passed over the ford Jabbok.* ²³*And he took them, and sent them over the brook, and sent over that he had.* ²⁴*And Jacob was left alone; and there wrestled a man with him until the breaking of the day.* ²⁵*And when he saw that* *he prevailed not against him, he touched the hollow of his thigh; and the hollow of Jacob's thigh was out of joint, as he wrestled with him. ²⁶And he said, Let me go, for the day breaketh. And he said, I will not let thee go, except thou bless me. ²⁷And he said unto him, What is thy name? And he said, Jacob. ²⁸And he said, Thy name shall be called no more Jacob, but Israel: for as a prince hast thou power with God and with men, and hast prevailed. ²⁹And Jacob asked him, and said, Tell me, I pray thee, thy name. And he said, Wherefore is it that thou dost ask after my name? And he blessed him there. ³⁰And Jacob called the name of the place* **Peniel***: for I have seen God face to face, and my life is preserved. ³¹And as he passed over Penuel the sun rose upon him, and he halted upon his thigh. ³²Therefore the children of Israel eat not of the sinew which shrank, which is upon the hollow of the thigh, unto this day: because he touched the hollow of Jacob's thigh in the sinew that shrank.*

(Descartes suggested that the pineal gland is "the seat of the soul" for several reasons. First, the soul is unitary, and unlike many areas of the brain the pineal gland appeared to be unitary (though subsequent microscopic inspection has revealed it is formed of two hemispheres).

### Great Tribulation

Twenty years later throughout the Middle East a severe famine occurred like none other that lasted seven years. It crippled nations. The word was that the only kingdom prospering was Egypt. In the second year of this great famine, when Israel (Jacob) was about 130 years old, he told his 10 sons of Leah, Bilhah and Zilpah to go to Egypt and buy grain. Israel's youngest son, Benjamin, born from Rachel, stayed behind by his father's order to keep him safe (Genesis 42:1-5).

When the 10 sons returned to their father Israel from Egypt, they were stockpiled with grain on their donkeys. They relayed to their father all that had happened in Egypt. They spoke of being accused of as spies and that their brother Simeon, had been taken prisoner. When Reuben, the eldest, mentioned that they needed to bring Benjamin to

Egypt to prove their word as honest men, their father became furious with them. He couldn't understand how they were put in a position to tell the Egyptians all about their family. When the sons of Israel opened their sacks, they saw their money that they used to pay for the grain. It was still in their possession, and so they all became afraid. Israel then became angry with the loss of Joseph, Simeon and now possibly Benjamin (Genesis 42:26-38).

It turned out that Joseph, who identified his brothers in Egypt, was able to secretly return that money that they used to pay for the grain, back to them. When the house of Israel consumed all the grain that they brought from Egypt, Israel told his sons to go back and buy more. This time, Judah spoke to his father in order to persuade him about having Benjamin accompany them, so as to prevent Egyptian retribution. In hopes of retrieving Simeon and ensuring Benjamin's return, Israel told them to bring the best fruits of their land, including balm, honey, spices, myrrh, pistachio, nuts and almonds. Israel also mentioned that the money that was returned to their money sacks was probably a mistake or an oversight on their part. So, he told them to bring that money back and use double that amount to pay for the new grain. Lastly, he let Benjamin go with them and said, "May God Almighty give you mercy . . . If I am bereaved, I am bereaved!" (Genesis 43:1-14),

en.wikipedia.org/wiki/Jacob

Jacob was manifesting using his seed (soul) as he reviewed the past; he let go of what he didn't want to change and created what he wanted. With a life review of the past, he was able to see what went right and what went wrong during his life experiences using the treasures in the kingdom. Notice the review was also reviewed with other seeds/souls (his sons).

## Jacob in the Old Kingdom

Jacob's life review manifesting created abundance beyond his imagination.

When the sons of Israel (Jacob) returned to Hebron from their second trip, they came back with 20 additional donkeys carrying all kinds of goods and supplies as well as Egyptian transport wagons. When their father came out to meet them, his sons told him that Joseph was still alive, that he was the governor over all of Egypt, and that he wanted the house of Israel to move to Egypt. Israel's heart "stood still" and just couldn't believe what he was hearing. Looking upon the wagons, he declared, "Joseph my son is still alive. I will go and see him before I die" (Genesis 45:16-28).

Israel and his entire house of 70 gathered up with all their livestock and began their journey to Egypt. En route, Israel stopped at Beersheba for the night to make a sacrificial offering to his god, Yahweh. Apparently he had some reservations about leaving the land of his forefathers, but God reassured him not to fear that he would rise again. God also assured that he would be with him, he would prosper, and he would also see his son Joseph who would lay him to rest. Continuing their journey to Egypt, when they approached in proximity, Israel sent his son Judah ahead to find out where the caravans were to stop. They were directed to disembark at Goshen. It was here, after 22 years, that Jacob saw his son Joseph once again. They embraced each other and wept together for quite a while. Israel then said, "Now let me die, since I have seen your face, because you are still alive" (Genesis 46:1-30).

The time had come for Joseph's family to personally meet the Pharaoh of Egypt. After Joseph prepared his family for the meeting, the brothers came before the Pharaoh first, formally requesting to pasture in Egyptian lands. The Pharaoh honored their stay and even made the notion that if there were any competent men in their house, then they may elect a chief herdsman to oversee Egyptian livestock. Finally, Joseph's father was brought out to meet the Pharaoh. Because the Pharaoh had such a high regard for Joseph, practically making him his equal, it was an honor to meet his father. Thus, Israel was able to bless the Pharaoh. The two chatted for a bit, the Pharaoh even inquiring of Israel's age, which happened to be 130 years old at that time. After the meeting, the families were directed to pasture in the land of Ramses where they lived in the province of Goshen. The house of Israel acquired many possessions and multiplied exceedingly during the course of 17 years, even through the worst of the seven-year famine (Genesis 46:31-47:28).

en.wikipedia.org

Using "oil" to nourish the "seed" will create greener pastures.

## *Jacob's Blessing*

**Ephesians 1:9-10 (KJV)**
*⁹Having made known unto us the mystery of his will, according to his good pleasure which he hath purposed in himself: ¹⁰That in the dispensation of the fulness of times he might gather together in one all things in Christ, both which are in heaven, and which are on earth; even in him:*

## Chapter V

# CHANGING OF THE GUARDS

### *Awareness*

Israel (Jacob) was 147 years old when he called to his favorite son Joseph and pleaded that he not be buried in Egypt. Rather, he requested to be carried to the land of Canaan to be buried with his forefathers. Joseph swore to do as his father asked of him. Not too long afterward, Israel had fallen ill, losing much of his vision. When Joseph came to visit his father, he brought with him his two sons, Ephraim and Manasseh. Israel declared that they would be heirs to the inheritance of the house of Israel, as if they were his own children, just as Reuben and Simeon were.

### *Acceptance*

Then Israel laid his right hand on the younger Ephraim's head and his left hand on the eldest Manasseh's head and blessed Joseph. However, Joseph was displeased that his father's right hand was not on the head of his firstborn, so he switched his father's hands. But Israel refused, saying, "but truly his younger brother shall be greater than he." A declaration he made, just as Israel himself was to his firstborn brother Esau. Then Israel called all of his sons in and prophesied their blessings or curses to all 12 of them in order of their ages (Genesis 47:29-49:32).

## *Transition*

Afterward, Israel died and the family, including the Egyptians, mourned him 70 days. Israel was embalmed and a great ceremonial journey to Canaan was prepared by Joseph. He led the servants of the Pharaoh and the elders of the houses of Israel and Egypt beyond the Jordan River to Atad where they observed seven days of mourning. Their lamentation was so great that it caught the attention of surrounding Canaanites, who remarked, "This is a deep mourning of the Egyptians."

The blessing, funeral procession and burying of Jacob are symbolic of bringing Jacob home again.

## Chapter VI

# SEALED WITH A KISS

*"Though we gotta say goodbye for the summer, baby, I promise you this, I'll send you all my love every day in a letter, sealed with a kiss."—* **Bobby Vinton, singer and songwriter**

As do messages repeat from lifetime to lifetime, so does history repeat over and over again—notably, in many of the ancient texts you will notice the request of returning the bones to the homeland, just to give you an example.

What happens when you send a message to someone and because they didn't respond, you know or think it wasn't received? You review the message and the process used to send it and then you send another message—bigger, better, clearer and louder than the message sent the time before. You will send it over and over again using different words or different tools, eager that the message will get to the destination and be received in full context and sometimes "sealed with a kiss".

We are the 12 Tribes of Jacob/IS:RA:EL/Mother/Father/God. In a manner of speaking, we have been separated from 10 of the tribes since birth—until "death do us part" or until we wake up!. Jacob had 12 sons and one daughter—the first 10 sons born to Jacob are the 10 lost tribes. They are hidden in the North—separated from us when our soul enters our physical body on this earth plane in the 3$^{rd}$ dimension.

The physical body where your soul resides matches our Mother/Earth's vibration, this is the DNA part that is understood by science.

The parts, "the 10 lost tribes", is the other DNA. The DNA that is not being used because it has been separated, covered up with leaves from the Garden of Eden is the spiritual DNA. It is the DNA scientists call "junk" DNA. They know it is there, but have no idea what it does or why it is there, yet☺. Without the use of this DNA, we are not operating with "olive" our faculties. We as spiritual beings having a human experience are limited to what we can do without them. It is high time to take off our leaves and reveal who we are!

We have enough wear-with-all in place to know to ask ourselves and sometimes each other the same questions over and over again. Doesn't it seem odd that no one is talking about the answers? With every question, there is an answer.

Who Am I and Where Did I come from? How did I get here and How do I get back home? It seems that maybe we have something in common with the rest of the world, including the "Ten Lost Tribes of Israel". It would make sense to say that "olive" us have the same soul purpose.

## A Soul Purpose

The founder of these lost tribes is also the founder of a "multitude of nations".

**Revelation 7:9 (KJV)**
*⁹After this I beheld, and, lo, a great multitude, which no man could number, of all nations, and kindreds, and people, and tongues, stood before the throne, and before the Lamb, clothed with white robes, and palms in their hands;*

**Genesis 17:4-5 (KJV)**
*⁴As for me, behold, my covenant is with thee, and thou shalt be a father of many nations. ⁵Neither shall thy name any more be called Abram, but thy name shall be Abraham; for a father of many nations have I made thee.*

The "Holy Grail" is with you and you shall be the father of many nations. The message is speaking to "olive" us.

**Genesis 48:10-19 (KJV)**
*10Now the eyes of Israel were dim for age, so that he could not see. And he brought them near unto him; and he kissed them, and embraced them. 11And Israel said unto Joseph, I had not thought to see thy face: and, lo, God hath shewed me also thy seed. 12And Joseph brought them out from between his knees, and he bowed himself with his face to the earth. 13And Joseph took them both, Ephraim in his right hand toward Israel's left hand, and Manasseh in his left hand toward Israel's right hand, and brought them near unto him. 14And Israel stretched out his right hand, and laid it upon Ephraim's head, who was the younger, and his left hand upon Manasseh's head, guiding his hands wittingly; for Manasseh was the firstborn. 15And he blessed Joseph, and said, God, before whom my fathers Abraham and Isaac did walk, the God which fed me all my life long unto this day, 16The Angel which redeemed me from all evil, bless the lads; and let my name be named on them, and the name of my fathers Abraham and Isaac; and let them grow into a multitude in the midst of the earth. 17And when Joseph saw that his father laid his right hand upon the head of Ephraim, it displeased him: and he held up his father's hand, to remove it from Ephraim's head unto Manasseh's head. 18And Joseph said unto his father, Not so, my father: for this is the firstborn; put thy right hand upon his head. 19And his father refused, and said, I know it, my son, I know it: he also shall become a people, and he also shall be great: but truly his younger brother shall be greater than he, and his seed shall become a multitude of nations.*

## The Twelve (12) Sons/Tribes of Jacob/Israel

**The 10 Lost Tribes of Israel/Jacob in the north (the Kingdom of Heaven)** were not lost, but hidden from deaf ears and blind eyes by those who have not found "The Kingdom of Heaven within The Holy Book of The Great Invisible Spirit" ☺. This DNA/blueprint is encoded within every soul—the biggest part of your DNA/blueprint that carries the majority of your unique God-given gifts and abilities separated or taken away from you at birth.

These gifts and abilities are created and enriched over your many lifetimes, your soul journey. The 10 tribes are always with you; you have not been aware or conscious of them until NOW because they are invisible. With each incarnation, we all start our new lives over again with a new set of possibilities and probabilities to gain experiences with one common, collective goal. While at the same time with the experiences we learn, the soul grows and retains the knowledge and information yet is not aware because man is sleeping.

**The Two (2) Tribes of Israel are in the south (the lower land)**—your physical body, easily accessed in the lower dimension, such as the third-dimensional Earth plane. These tribes are the tribes you are aware of (conscious of); they are not lost or hidden. These are what every human being has been operating with—a basic computer-operating system. This is the part of the DNA that matches up with your physical family from both your birth mother and father.

**The Ten (10) Tribes of Israel are in the north**—your spiritual body (The Kingdom of Heaven), accessed through "the Holy Book within The Great Invisible Spirit☺". This is accessible to those who want to reclaim their gifts and abilities through a spiritual transformation, letting go of old beliefs, systems and negative energy that no longer belong to you and no longer serve you.

No one can take these away from you; even though it seems you are separated from these tribes, the truth is they have always been there waiting for your acknowledgement. Where you go, they go. They are part of you and you are part of them. Some souls come into physical bodies with more abilities than others because this is what was agreed upon before the incarnation.☺

The new fifth-dimensional energies are now available, making it possible to upgrade the DNA that we haven't been using, allowing a quickening to occur. The DNA has been sitting there available, ready for use but yet unused for eons. There is a reason for everything. It may be very difficult to navigate with the waves of new energy if your vibration doesn't match that of the new frequencies on the "New Earth".

It is the DNA that our spiritual being has carried from lifetime to lifetime—our God-given birthright that is hidden by a veil upon the second we are born into the third-dimensional energies on Earth. During this exact time at birth, we are each given "Free Will and Choice" to do as we wish—just the same way Eve did when she ate the forbidden fruit. For the most part, as children we grow up guided by our parents and leaders of the religious, education and government institutions that we are exposed to. Very few stray very far from the sidewalk due to fear, worry, comfort and other lower level feelings a human being endures during a lifetime.

Once a soul is aware and has accepted his divine identity, the transformation, a rebirth process begins to bring these tribes home—bring Jacob home. Individually, we must each match our own vibration with that of the "New Earth" in order to reach the "Kingdom of Heaven".

The way to the "Kingdom of Heaven" is by creating a pathway within "The Holy Book". Understand that no two pathways are the same—you cannot do it for others. Each individual has his own lessons before he can become a master. We can simply guide others, showing the way, being a light.

This is an individual spiritual journey, however when we help ourselves, we help others and that mirrors back to when we help others, we also help ourselves.

"The Holy Book" (The Holy Grail) is the "Heart" within "The Great Invisible Spirit".

"The Great Invisible Spirit" is "YOU". ☺

You are a spiritual being having a human experience. Your soul, has incarnated many times into physical form sometimes referred to as your "tent". Our spirit form is the vessel our soul resides when we are not in another form such as the human body.

Once you get to the Kingdom of Heaven within The Holy Book, you will be reconnected with the multitude of nations—your coat of many colours.

## *Bring Jacob Home Again*

### Twelve Tribes of Jacob/Israel

Each tribe has 12 blueprints/DNA (12 X 12) = 144 blueprints

The molecules in the energy of the blueprints correspond to the molecules of the energy of the elements. I happen to know that Tesla and Einstein have both come back with their messages, too. ☺

The Great Cycle of Nineveh: The 144 elements of the Periodic Table correspond to certain energies, similar patterning when broken down on an energy level.

**Nineveh** is the capital of Assyria, built by Nimrod (Genesis 10:10). It's also the city to which Jonah was sent (Jonah 1:2).

**Genesis 10:8 (KJV)**
*⁸And Cush begat Nimrod: he began to be a mighty one in the earth.*

**Nineveh:** (*nin*) means offspring, from the root (*nun*) meaning spread, circulate, grow, increase. (*naweh*) means dwelling, from the root (*nawa*) meaning keep at home.

**Nimrod** is a son of Cush, son of Ham, son of Noah (Genesis 10:8). Nimrod is a mighty king, and the first active character after the flood cycle.

**Nimrod's** meaning to be rebellious, rebel, revolt occurs about 25 times in the Bible, half of which cover scenes in which man revolts against man (and always Israel and its king revolting against an invaded or occupying foreign force), and in the other half man revolts against God.

## Fig Tree Leaf Taken from Nimrod

On the day of Abraham's death, Esau had been out in the fields as usual. (Esau was a spiritual man who when he was out in the fields, he was connecting to spirit.) He had lost his way and was trying to find his way back (he was having some inner struggles),when King Nimrod (King rebellion) arrived with two servants (witnesses or attendants). Esau hid behind a rock (Esau went within) and when Nimrod was left unguarded, he killed him and fought the two servants who rushed to the aid of their master. Esau escaped with King Nimrod's clothes. (Esau fought an inner battle and came out of it unscathed.) These were Adam's garments (leaves) which later became the property of Noah; Noah's son Ham, who was Nimrod's grandfather, had subsequently become their owner, and finally Nimrod had acquired them. These divine clothes had made Nimrod a powerful and skillful hunter and a mighty ruler over all other kings. Now Esau had come into possession of the most valuable and cherished property a hunter could desire. The messages have been repeated over many lifetimes, over history.

**Jonah 4:11 (KJV)**
*[11]And should not I spare **Nineveh**, that great city, wherein are more than sixscore thousand persons that cannot discern between their right hand and their left hand; and also much cattle?* (the masses who don't know the difference yet)

## The Two Tribes in the South are not Hidden

They are separated at birth from the other 10 tribes who are lost, hidden under the veil. They are there, but you are not aware of them. If you are aware of them, have you accepted them? They are the unused part of your DNA. They are our divine blueprint. A "reconnection" is required through a spiritual transformation to make a path to reclaim your true identity/divinity—your divine blueprint.

After the life reviews among the souls, the path has been altered somewhat to ensure the results are achieved without outside intruders. Help is being poured onto the Earth plane as the Earth goes into accelerated evolution.

To help and guide "olive" us through this final phase in the battle between good and evil, the Great Brotherhood of Light has been approaching ever closer the Earth plane, providing it with adepts and initiates who are their disciples, all working together under a grand divine plan. As these high beings mix with the earthly populations, less and less shall there be the apparent distance and separation between the lost tribes of ISRAEL (Mother-Father-God).

More and more, we will notice and receive the messages put on our paths. All parts of our individual lives and our collective existence on Earth will be influenced by the Great Brotherhood of Light, bringing messages in many forms, which is all part of the grand plan to bring about the New Golden Age.

# PART IV

# The Great Invisible Spirit

**Colossians 1:15-16** (KJV)
[15] Who is the image of the invisible God, the firstborn of every creature:16 For by him were all things created, that are in heaven, and that are in earth, visible and invisible, whether they be thrones, or dominions, or principalities, or powers: all things were created by him, and for him:

*Chapter 9*

# I AM, GREATER THAN EVER

I AM, greater than ever; I AM, greater today than yesterday, and I will be even greater tomorrow.

As we go through life, something inside of us strives to achieve advancement in many ways. It is in us—it is our nature to try to improve or become better in order to achieve our goals. We try it this way, and then we try it that way. Then we try it again the other way, because the first way was better than the second way. At the end of the day, the way we think works best is the way we move forward on our path.

Some may have individual goals, along with goals that require others to participate to get the desired result. During the process, we often take on more responsibility to gain more knowledge and wisdom. When we reach the desired goal, we set new goals. "olive" us have the same goal—that goal is achieving the desired results we have carefully planned out.

Sometimes, things get in our way. If negative thoughts like worry, fear, hatred or greed show up in the process, these energies will set you back and block you from achieving your goals. During the review, you will need to see if these road blocks are stopping you in your tracks or turning you around to a destination unknown.

## *Elijah*

Elijah knew who he was. He knew what his plan and purpose was, too. He also knew who he made the plans with. Each time Elijah reincarnated, he was better than the time before.

**Elijah,** meaning "Yahweh is my God", was a prophet in the Kingdom of Samaria during the reign of Ahab (9th century BCE), according to the Books of Kings.

**Elijah's return is prophesied "before the coming of the great and terrible day of the Lord" Malachi 4:5—(KJV). Yahweh is the name of God in the Bible, the God of Abraham, Isaac, Jacob, Jews and Christians.**

The traditional rendering of the name, as found in English Bibles, is **"I am who I am" or "I am that I am"**.

The Bible describes Yahweh as the god who delivered IS-RA-EL (Mother-Father-God) from Egypt (his kingdom) and gave the Ten Commandments.

*Romans 13:8-10 KJV*
*⁸ Owe no man anything, but to love one another: for he that loveth another hath fulfilled the law. 9 For this, Thou shalt not commit adultery, Thou shalt not kill, Thou shalt not steal, Thou shalt not bear false witness, Thou shalt not covet; and if there be any other commandment, it is briefly comprehended in this saying, namely, Thou shalt love thy neighbour as thyself. 10 Love worketh no ill to his neighbour: therefore love is the fulfilling of the law.*

**The Bible also states that Yahweh revealed himself to ISRAEL as a god who would not permit his people to make idols or worship other gods. "I am the Lord: that is my name: and my glory will I not give to another, neither my praise to graven images." Isaiah 42:8 (KJV)**

**Malachi 4 (KJV)**
*"For behold, the day cometh that shall burn as an oven, and all the proud, yea, and all that do wickedly shall burn as stubble; for they that come shall burn them, saith the Lord of Hosts, that it shall leave them neither root nor branch."*

(The burning signifies getting rid of what no longer serves your spiritual being.)

*"Behold, I will reveal unto you the Priesthood, by the hand of Elijah the prophet, before the coming of the great and dreadful day of the Lord." "And he shall plant in the hearts of the children the promises made to the fathers, and the hearts of the children shall turn to their fathers. If it were not so, the whole Earth would be utterly wasted at his coming."*

*The above scripture is worth analyzing for the sake of understanding. With a different set of eyes and ears, the truth will be revealed— truly a spiritual transformation. It may seem difficult to wrap your pineal gland around at the moment.* ☺

*"For behold, the day cometh that shall burn as an oven, and all the proud, yea, and all that do wickedly shall burn as stubble;* (the day is coming that you will be proud that what you have done wickedly will burn away as stubble, getting rid of what does not serve you anymore.) *for they that come shall burn them, saith the Lord of Hosts, that it shall leave them neither root nor branch."* (for those who come shall come to the Kingdom of Heaven burning away the sins—the karma—and it shall leave nothing there. In other words, that it shall leave them a clean slate—a New Beginning, A New Earth, A New Way of Living, A New Human. ☺)

*"Behold, I will reveal unto you the Priesthood, by the hand of Elijah the prophet, before the coming of the great and dreadful day of the Lord.* (Elijah will reveal to us the Holy ones before the great and dreadful day.)

*"And he shall plant in the hearts of the children the promises made to the fathers, and the hearts of the children shall turn to their fathers. If it were not so, the whole Earth would be utterly wasted at his coming. (Elijah will come back to make things right—showing the son of man that we are all part of God. We have lost our identity but now are found. If this wasn't true, there is no sense in his coming because the son of man and the Earth would be wasted and, therefore, his coming would be for nothing.)*

Elijah has returned a better and greater Elijah with a clearer and stronger message than the time before and the time before that. He is bigger, greater, stronger, smarter and more powerful than ever. He is in balance with the new energies here on the Earth.

Elijah in a previous life started the process of our separation and now it is time for him to turn things around, make things right again. ***His vibration matches that of the higher frequencies available at this time in history.***

**1 Corinthians 2:11-16 (KJV)**
*[11]For what man knoweth the things of a man, save* **the spirit of man which is in him?** *even so the things of God knoweth no man, but the Spirit of God.* *[12]***Now we have received, not the spirit of the world, but the spirit which is of God; that we might know the things that are freely given to us of God.** *[13]Which things also we speak, not in the words which man's wisdom teacheth, but which the Holy Ghost teacheth; comparing spiritual things with spiritual. [14]But the natural man receiveth not the things of the Spirit of God: for they are foolishness unto him: neither can he know them, because they are spiritually discerned. [15]But he that is spiritual judgeth all things, yet he himself is judged of no man. [16]For who hath known the mind of the Lord, that he may instruct him? but we have the mind of Christ.*

## Widow of Zarephath

Elijah's name was the golden key that unlocked the doorway of the code of colors, allowing me in this life to receive and **know** the messages that were starting to pour into my vessel. As I weaved the little bits and pieces of light together, the story began to energize.

The widow was clairsentient, living in desperate times with her son, Jonah. She *knew* Elijah when he came because he was family—soul family. Together, they made a daily feast (manifest) with the unlimited amount of "oil" (our will) and grain (seed) that was miraculously made available.

After Elijah's confrontation with Ahab, God told him to flee out of Israel, to a hiding place by the brook Cherith, east of the Jordan, where he would be fed by ravens. When the brook dried up, God sent him to a widow living in the town of Zarephatho in Phoenicia.

It has been written that when Elijah found the widow and asked to be fed, she said that she did not have sufficient food to keep her and her own son alive. Elijah told her that **God would not allow her supply of flour or oil to run out**, saying, "Don't be afraid—this is what the Lord, the God of Israel, says: 'The jar of flour will not be used up and the jug of **oil** (our will), will not run dry until the day the Lord gives rain on the land.'" God gave her "manna" from heaven even while he was withholding food from his unfaithful people in the "promised land".

**Manna** was the name of an edible substance that God provided for the Israelites during their travels in the desert, according to the Bible. ☺

When Adam was dying, Eve and Seth went to the garden to get "oil" from the Tree of Life. Seth *knew* his father's oil had run out and when he got to the garden, Archangel Michael told them that it was Adam's time to go—it was his choice to go, it was his time to go.

### Numbers 11:7-9 (KJV)
*[7]And the manna was as coriander seed, and the colour thereof as the colour of bdellium. [8]And the people went about, and gathered it, and ground it in mills, or beat it in a mortar, and baked it in pans, and made cakes of it: and the taste of it was as the taste of fresh oil. [9]And when the dew fell upon the camp in the night, the manna fell upon it.*

Manna is described as tasting like fresh oil. Manna is angel's food.

**Psalm 78:25 (KJV)**
*25Man did eat angels' food: he sent them meat to the full.*

## *Elijah saves Jonah*

Sometime later, the widow's son died and the widow cried, "Did you come to remind me of my sin and kill my son?" Elijah prayed that God might restore her son so that the truth and trustworthiness of God's word might be demonstrated. ***1Kings 17:22*** relates how God, "heard the voice of Elijah; and the soul of the child came into him again, and he revived." This is the first instance of raising the dead recorded in scripture. Jonah had a near-death experience.

After more than three years of drought and famine, God told Elijah to return to Ahab and announce the end of the drought. This was not to be occasioned by repentance in Israel but by the command of the Lord, who had determined to reveal himself again to his people. While on his way, Elijah met Obadiah, the head of Ahab's household, who had hidden a hundred prophets of the God of Israel when Ahab and Jezebel had been killing them. Elijah sent Obadiah back to Ahab to announce his return to Israel.

When Ahab confronted Elijah, he referred to him as the "troubler of Israel." Elijah responded by throwing the charge back at Ahab, saying that it was Ahab who had troubled Israel by allowing the worship of false gods. Elijah then scolded both the people of Israel and Ahab for their agreement in Baal worship. "How long will you go limping with two different opinions? If the Lord is God, follow him; but if Baal then follow him" (***Kings 18:21***).

At this point, Elijah proposed a direct test of the powers of Baal and Yahweh. The people of Israel, 450 prophets of Baal and 400 prophets of Asherah were summoned to Mount Carmel. Two altars were built, one for Baal and one for Yahweh. Wood was laid on the altars. Two oxen were slaughtered and cut into pieces; the pieces were laid on the wood. Elijah then invited the priests of Baal to pray for fire to light the sacrifice. They prayed from morning to noon without success. Elijah ridiculed their efforts. They responded by cutting themselves and adding their own blood to the sacrifice (such mutilation of the body was strictly forbidden in Mosaic law). They continued praying until evening without success.

Elijah now ordered that the altar of Yahweh be drenched with water from "four large jars" poured three times (***1 Kings 18:33-34***). He asked God to accept the sacrifice. Fire fell from the sky, consuming the water, the sacrifice and the stones of the altar itself as well. Elijah seized the moment and orders the death of the prophets of Baal. Elijah prayed earnestly for rain to fall again on the land. Then the rains began, signaling **the end** of the famine.

*"The emotional body is fueled by the Element of Water—the mental body provides the seed thoughts and the Emotional body fuels the E-motion or energy in motion."—****Ronna Herman via Archangel Michael***

## *Why Are You Here?*

According to Wikipedia, Jezebel, enraged that Elijah had ordered the deaths of her priests, threatened to kill Elijah (***Kings 19:1-13***). This was Elijah's first encounter with Jezebel and not the last. Later, Elijah would prophesy about Jezebel's death because of her sin. Later, Elijah fled to Beersheba in Judah, continued alone into the wilderness, and finally sat down under a juniper tree, praying for death (sleep). He fell asleep under the tree; then an angel touched him and told him to wake and eat. When he awoke, he found **bread** and a jar of water. He ate, drank, and went back to sleep. The angel came a second time and told him to eat and drink because he had a **long journey** ahead of him.

Elijah traveled for 40 days and 40 nights to Mount Horeb (the mountain of gods) where Moses had received the Torah (instruction or teaching). Elijah was the first and only person described in the

Bible as going back to Horeb after Moses and his generation had left Horeb several centuries before. He sought shelter in a cave. God again spoke to Elijah (*1 Kings 19:9*): "What doest thou here, Elijah?" Elijah did not give a direct answer to the Lord's question, but evaded and spoke vaguely, implying that **the work the Lord had begun centuries earlier** had now come to nothing and that his own work was fruitless—unlike Moses, who tried to defend Israel when they sinned with the golden calf.

The **golden calf** was an idol made by Aaron to satisfy the Israelites during Moses' absence, when he went up to Mount Sinai. The calf was intended to be a physical representation of the God of Israel and, therefore, was doubly wrong for involving Israel in idolatry and for ascribing physicality to God. The incident is known as "The Sin of the Calf".

Elijah bitterly complained over the Israelites' unfaithfulness and said he is the "only one left". Up until this time, Elijah had only the word of God to guide him, but now he was told to go outside the cave and "stand before the Lord." A terrible wind passed, but God was not in the wind. A great earthquake shook the mountain, but God was not in the earthquake. Then a fire passed the mountain, but God was not in the fire. Then **a "still, small voice" came to Elijah** and asked again, "What doest thou here, Elijah?" Elijah again evaded the question and his grief was unchanged, showing that he did not understand the importance of the divine revelation he had just witnessed. God then sent him out again, this time to Damascus to anoint Hazael as king of Syria, Jehu as King of Israel and Elisha as his replacement.

## *Trading Places*

Elijah, in company with Elisha, approached the Jordan. He rolled up his robe and struck the water (*2 Kings 2:8*). The water immediately divided and Elijah and Elisha crossed on dry land. Suddenly, a chariot of fire and horses of fire appeared and Elijah was lifted up in a whirlwind. As Elijah was lifted up, his mantle (robe) fell to the ground and Elisha picked it up. Just the same way as Adam and Eve cover themselves when they descended into the 3rd dimension—Elijah uncovers himself upon his ascension, trading places from physical form to spirit form for his soul to reside.

**Elijah** was mentioned once more in 2 Chronicles 21, which was his final mention in the Hebrew Bible. A letter was sent under the prophet's name to Jehoram of Judah. It told him that he had led the people of Judah astray in the same way that Israel was led astray. The prophet ended the letter with a prediction of a painful death. **This letter is a puzzle to readers** for several reasons. **First**, it concerns a king of the southern kingdom, while Elijah concerned himself with the kingdom of Israel.

**Elijah,** the "kingdom of IS-RA-EL", is where we all belong. The letter was sent to the leader of one of the tribes that had strayed away from the other tribes. Elijah's mission was to save lost sheep—bring them back together, back to mother-father-god. The southern kingdom was none other than the lower land—the lowest dimension in the Universe where the son of man and the Earth had been experiencing and learning the hard way.

**Matthew 18:12-14 (KJV)**
*¹²How think ye? if a man have an hundred sheep, and one of them be gone astray, doth he not leave the ninety and nine, and goeth into the mountains, and seeketh that which is gone astray? ¹³And if so be that he find it, verily I say unto you, he rejoiceth more of that sheep, than of the ninety and nine which went not astray. ¹⁴Even so it is not the will of your Father which is in heaven, that one of these little ones should perish.*

*Malachi 4:5-6*
*Behold, I will send you Elijah the prophet before the great and terrible day of the Lord comes. And he will turn the hearts of fathers to their children and the hearts of children to their fathers, lest I come and smite the land with a curse.*

Some believe Jesus said that John the Baptist was Elijah, who would come before the "great and terrible day" as predicted by Malachi.

**Matthew 11:7-15 (KJV)**
*⁷And as they departed, Jesus began to say unto the multitudes concerning John, What went ye out into the wilderness to see? A reed shaken with the wind? ⁸But what went ye out for to see? A man clothed in soft raiment? behold, they that wear soft clothing are in kings' houses. ⁹But what went ye out for to see? A prophet? yea, I say unto you, and more than a prophet. ¹⁰For this is he, of whom it is written, Behold, I send my messenger before thy face, which shall prepare thy way before thee. ¹¹Verily I say unto you, Among them that are born of women there hath not risen a greater than John the Baptist: notwithstanding he that is least in the kingdom of heaven is greater than he. ¹²And from the days of John the Baptist until now the kingdom of heaven suffereth violence, and the violent take it by force. ¹³For all the prophets and the law prophesied until John. ¹⁴And if ye will receive it, this is Elias, which was for to come. ¹⁵He that hath ears to hear, let him hear.*

# Chapter 99

# TRUTH

## Moses Reincarnated

**Deuteronomy 34:10 (KJV)**
*[10]And there arose not a prophet since in Israel like unto **Moses**, whom the LORD knew face to face*

**Luke 7:28 (KJV)**
*[28]For I say unto you, among those that are born of women there is not a greater prophet than **John the Baptist**: but he that is least in the kingdom of God is greater than he*

John the Baptist preached a message of repentance and baptism. He predicted the day of the judgment using imagery similar to that of Malachi. He also preached that the Messiah was coming. All of this was done in a style that immediately recalled the image of Elijah to his audience. He wore a coat of animal hair secured with a leather belt (***Matthew 3:4, Mark 1:6***). He also frequently preached in wilderness areas near the Jordan River.

He knew Elijah, and Elijah knew him—they were soul family. John came in the spirit of Elijah because Elijah knew Moses/John and Elijah gave John the power of his own spirit. Moses/John came again as one of the witnesses to pave the way for the third coming of the Christ. He has returned in this lifetime even better than he was in the vessels before. ☺

**Mark 1 (KJV)**
¹*The beginning of the gospel of Jesus Christ, the Son of God;* ²*As it is written in the prophets,* **Behold, I send my messenger before thy face, which shall prepare thy way before thee.** ³**The voice of one crying in the wilderness, Prepare ye the way of the Lord, make his paths straight** (one who is on the spiritual path). ⁴*John did baptize in the wilderness, and preach the baptism of repentance for the remission of sins.* ⁵*And there went out unto him all the land of Judaea, and they of Jerusalem, and were all baptized of him in the river of Jordan, confessing their sins.* ⁶*And John was clothed with camel's hair, and with a girdle of a skin about his loins; and he did eat locusts and wild honey;*

⁷*And preached, saying,* **There cometh one mightier than I after me, the latchet of whose shoes I am not worthy to stoop down and unloose.** ⁸*I indeed have baptized you with water: but he shall baptize you with the Holy Ghost* (the emotional body fueled by the Element of Water). ⁹*And it came to pass in those days, that Jesus came from Nazareth of Galilee, and was baptized of John in Jordan.* ¹⁰*And straightway coming up out of the water, he saw the heavens opened, and the Spirit like a dove descending upon him:* ¹¹*And there came a voice from heaven, saying, Thou art my beloved Son, in whom I am well pleased.*

¹²**And immediately the spirit driveth him into the wilderness** (the field of higher consciousness). ¹³*And he was there in the wilderness forty days, tempted of Satan; and was with the wild beasts; and the angels ministered unto him.*

¹⁴*Now after that John was put in prison, Jesus came into Galilee, preaching the gospel of the kingdom of God,* ¹⁵*And saying, The time is fulfilled, and the kingdom of God is at hand: repent ye, and believe the gospel.*

¹⁶*Now as he walked by the sea of Galilee, he saw Simon and Andrew his brother casting a net into the sea: for they were fishers.* ¹⁷*And Jesus said unto them, Come ye after me, and I will make you to become fishers of men.* ¹⁸*And straightway they forsook their nets, and followed him.*

¹⁹And when he had gone a little farther thence, he saw James the son of Zebedee, and John his brother, who also were in the ship mending their nets. ²⁰And straightway he called them: and they left their father Zebedee in the ship with the hired servants, and went after him. ²¹And they went into Capernaum; and straightway on the sabbath day he entered into the synagogue, and taught. ²²And they were astonished at his doctrine: for he taught them as one that had authority, and not as the scribes.

²³**And there was in their synagogue a man with an unclean spirit**; and he cried out, ²⁴Saying, Let us alone; what have we to do with thee, thou Jesus of Nazareth? art thou come to destroy us? I know thee who thou art, the Holy One of God. ²⁵**And Jesus rebuked him, saying, Hold thy peace, and come out of him.** ²⁶**And when the unclean spirit had torn him, and cried with a loud voice, he came out of him.**

²⁷And they were all amazed, insomuch that they questioned among themselves, saying, What thing is this? what new doctrine is this? for with authority commandeth he even the unclean spirits, and they do obey him. ²⁸And immediately his fame spread abroad throughout all the region round about Galilee.

²⁹And forthwith, when they were come out of the synagogue, they entered into the house of Simon and Andrew, with James and John. ³⁰But Simon's wife's mother lay sick of a fever, and anon they tell him of her. ³¹**And he came and took her by the hand, and lifted her up; and immediately the fever left her, and she ministered unto them.** ³²**And at even, when the sun did set, they brought unto him all that were diseased, and them that were possessed with devils.**

³³And all the city was gathered together at the door. ³⁴And **he healed many that were sick of divers' diseases, and cast out many devils; and suffered not the devils to speak, because they knew him.** ³⁵And in the morning, rising up a great while before day, he went out, and departed into a solitary place, and there prayed. ³⁶And Simon and they that were with him followed after him. ³⁷And when they had found him, they said unto him, All men seek for thee.

³⁸*And he said unto them, Let us go into the next towns, that I may preach there also: for therefore came I forth.* ³⁹*And he preached in their synagogues throughout all Galilee, and cast out devils.* ⁴⁰**And there came a leper to him**, *beseeching him, and kneeling down to him, and saying unto him, If thou wilt, thou canst make me clean.*

⁴¹*And* **Jesus, moved with compassion, put forth his hand, and touched him**, *and saith unto him, I will; be thou clean.* ⁴²*And as soon as he had spoken, immediately the leprosy departed from him, and he was cleansed.* ⁴³*And he straitly charged him, and forthwith sent him away;*

⁴⁴*And saith unto him, See thou* **say nothing to any man**: *but* **go thy way, shew thyself to the priest, and offer for thy cleansing those things which Moses commanded, for a testimony unto them.** ⁴⁵**But he went out, and began to publish it much, and to blaze abroad the matter, insomuch that Jesus could no more openly enter into the city,** *but was without in desert places: and they came to him from every quarter.*

In the Gospel of John, John the Baptist was asked by a delegation of priests if he was Elijah, to which he replied, "I AM **not** (*John 1:21*)."

**John 1 (KJV)**
¹*In the beginning was the Word, and the Word was with God, and the Word was God.* ²*The same was in the beginning with God.* ³*All things were made by him; and without him was not any thing made that was made.* ⁴*In him was life; and the life was the light of men.* ⁵*And the light shineth in darkness; and the darkness comprehended it not.* ⁶**There was a man sent from God, whose name was John.** ⁷**The same came for a witness, to bear witness of the Light, that all men through him might believe.** ⁸**He was not that Light, but was sent to bear witness of that Light.** ⁹**That was the true Light, which lighteth every man that cometh into the world.** ¹⁰*He was in the world, and the world was made by him, and the world knew him not.* ¹¹*He came unto his own, and his own received him not.* ¹²*But as many as received him, to them gave he power to become the sons of God, even to them that believe on his name:* ¹³*Which were born, not of blood, nor of the will of the flesh, nor of the will of man, but of God.*

¹⁴*And the Word was made flesh, and dwelt among us, (and we beheld his glory, the glory as of the only begotten of the Father,) full of grace and truth.* ¹⁵*John bare witness of him, and cried, saying, This was he of whom I spake, He that cometh after me is preferred before me: for he was before me.* ¹⁶*And of his fulness have all we received, and grace for grace.*

¹⁷**For the law was given by Moses, but grace and truth came by Jesus Christ.** ¹⁸*No man hath seen God at any time, the only begotten Son, which is in the bosom of the Father, he hath declared him.* ¹⁹*And this is the record of John, when the Jews sent priests and Levites from Jerusalem to ask him, Who art thou?*

²⁰*And he confessed, and denied not; but confessed, I am not the Christ.* ²¹*And they asked him, What then?* **Art thou Elias? And he saith, I am not**. *Art thou that prophet? And he answered, No.* ²²*Then said they unto him, Who art thou? that we may give an answer to them that sent us. What sayest thou of thyself?* ²³**He said, I am the voice of one crying in the wilderness, Make straight the way of the Lord, as said the prophet Elias.**

²⁴*And they which were sent were of the Pharisees.* ²⁵*And they asked him, and said unto him, Why baptizest thou then, if thou be not that Christ, nor Elias, neither that prophet?* ²⁶*John answered them, saying, I baptize with water: but there standeth one among you, whom ye know not;* ²⁷*He it is, who coming after me is preferred before me, whose shoe's latchet I am not worthy to unloose.* ²⁸*These things were done in Bethabara beyond Jordan, where John was baptizing.*

John was guiding the others, as each had to use his own oil—we cannot use our oil to do the lessons for others.

²⁹*The next day John seeth Jesus coming unto him, and saith, Behold the Lamb of God, which taketh away the sin of the world.* ³⁰**This is he of whom I said, After me cometh a man which is preferred before me: for he was before me.** ³¹**And I knew him not:** *but that he should be made manifest to Israel, therefore am I come baptizing with water.*

No one knew Jesus when he was Elijah.

**³²And John bare record, saying, I saw the Spirit descending from heaven like a dove, and it abode upon him. ³³And I knew him not: but he that sent me to baptize with water, the same said unto me, Upon whom thou shalt see the Spirit descending, and remaining on him, the same is he which baptizeth with the Holy Ghost.**

*³⁴And I saw, and bare record that this is the Son of God. ³⁵Again the next day after John stood, and two of his disciples; ³⁶And looking upon Jesus as he walked, he saith, Behold the Lamb of God! ³⁷And the two disciples heard him speak, and they followed Jesus.*

*³⁸Then Jesus turned, and saw them following, and saith unto them, What seek ye? They said unto him, Rabbi, (which is to say, being interpreted, Master,) where dwellest thou? ³⁹He saith unto them, Come and see. They came and saw where he dwelt, and abode with him that day: for it was about the tenth hour. ⁴⁰One of the two which heard John speak, and followed him, was Andrew, Simon Peter's brother.*

*⁴¹He first findeth his own brother Simon, and saith unto him, We have found the Messias, which is, being interpreted, the Christ. ⁴²And he brought him to Jesus.* **And when Jesus beheld him, he said, Thou art Simon the son of Jona: thou shalt be called Cephas,** *which is by interpretation, a stone.*

*⁴³The day following Jesus would go forth into Galilee, and findeth Philip, and saith unto him, Follow me. ⁴⁴Now Philip was of Bethsaida, the city of Andrew and Peter. ⁴⁵Philip findeth Nathanael, and saith unto him,* **We have found him, of whom Moses in the law, and the prophets, did write, Jesus of Nazareth, the son of Joseph.**

*⁴⁶And Nathanael said unto him, Can there any good thing come out of Nazareth? Philip saith unto him, Come and see. ⁴⁷Jesus saw Nathanael coming to him, and saith of him, Behold an Israelite indeed, in whom is no guile! ⁴⁸Nathanael saith unto him, Whence knowest thou me? Jesus answered and said unto him, Before that Philip called thee, when thou* wast under the fig tree, I saw thee. ⁴⁹Nathanael answered and saith unto him, Rabbi, thou art the Son of God; thou art the King of Israel.

⁵⁰Jesus answered and said unto him, Because I said unto thee, I saw thee under the fig tree, believest thou? thou shalt see greater things than these. ⁵¹And he saith unto him, **Verily, verily, I say unto you, Hereafter ye shall see heaven open, and the angels of God ascending and descending upon the Son of man.**

## Elijah Reincarnated

In the Gospel of Luke, Herod Antipas heard some of the stories surrounding Jesus. Some told Herod that John the Baptist, whom he had executed, had come back to life. Others told him that it was Elijah. Later in the same gospel, Jesus asked his disciples who the people say that he is. The apostles' answers included Elijah among others.

Each incarnation we return to play out life experiences in many cases completely opposite of a previous lifetime. We must experience both negative and positive sides of the experiences to create the balancing of the karma and yin and yang.

Upon our return to spirit form, our life is reviewed with other soul family members, and we together determine what we could do differently, to achieve the required result. ☺ We get smarter and better as we accumulate the experience into our personalities.

During Jesus' crucifixion, some of the onlookers wondered if Elijah would come to rescue him, as by the time of Jesus, Elijah had entered folklore as a rescuer of Jews in distress.

## Transfiguration

Elijah made an appearance in the New Testament during an incident known as the Transfiguration. At the summit of an unnamed mount, Jesus' face began to shine. The disciples who were with Him heard the voice of God announce that Jesus is "My Beloved Son." The disciples also saw Moses and Elijah appear and talk with Jesus.

There is a consensus among Christian theologians that Elijah appeared as a witness of the prophets and Moses as a witness of the law for the divinely announced "Son of God."

\*\* Elijah is Jesus and Moses is John the Baptist. Moses came before Elijah and John came before Jesus to pave the way for the Messiah coming. They have all returned for the end of times—to bring Jacob home again.

Elijah is also mentioned three more times in the New Testament in Luke, Romans and James. In Luke 4:24-27, Jesus used Elijah as an example of rejected prophets. Jesus said, "No prophet is accepted in his own country," and then mentioned Elijah, saying that there were many widows in Israel, but Elijah was sent to one in Phoenicia. In Romans 11:1-6, **Paul cited Elijah as an example of God's never forsaking his people (the Israelites)**. In James 5:16-18, James said, "The effectual fervent prayer of a righteous man availeth much," and then cited Elijah's prayers that started and ended the famine in Israel as examples.

## Who Is Apostle Paul?

*Romans 11 (KJV)*
*¹ I say then, Hath God cast away his people? God forbid. For I also am an Israelite, of the seed of Abraham, of the tribe of Benjamin.*

**Paul the Apostle** (c. AD 5—c. AD 67; variously referred to as the "Apostle Paul" or "Saint Paul"), also known as **Saul of Tarsus**, is perhaps the most influential early Christian missionary.

According to the writings in the New Testament, Paul was known as Saul prior to his conversion and was dedicated to the persecution of the early disciples of Jesus in the area of Jerusalem. While traveling from Jerusalem to Damascus on a mission to "bring them which were there bound unto Jerusalem", the resurrected Jesus appeared to him in a great light. Saul was struck blind, but after three days his sight was restored by Ananias of Damascus, and Paul began to preach that Jesus of Nazareth was the Jewish Messiah and the Son of God.

**Acts 9:10-18 (KJV)**
*[10]And there was a certain disciple at Damascus, named Ananias; and to him said the Lord in a vision, Ananias. And he said, Behold, I am here, Lord. [11]And the Lord said unto him, Arise, and go into the street which is called Straight, and enquire in the house of Judas for one called Saul, of Tarsus: for, behold, he prayeth, [12]And hath seen in a vision a man named Ananias coming in, and putting his hand on him, that he might receive his sight. [13]Then Ananias answered, Lord,* ***I have heard by many of this man, how much evil he hath done to thy saints at Jerusalem:*** *[14]****And here he hath authority from the chief priests to bind all that call on thy name.***

*[15]But the Lord said unto him, Go thy way: for* ***he is a chosen vessel unto me, to bear my name before the Gentiles, and kings, and the children of Israel:*** *[16]For I will shew him how great things he must suffer for my name's sake. [17]And Ananias went his way, and entered into the house; and putting his hands on him said, Brother Saul, the Lord, even Jesus, that appeared unto thee in the way as thou camest, hath sent me, that thou mightest receive thy sight, and be filled with the Holy Ghost. [18]And immediately there fell from his eyes as it had been scales: and he received sight forthwith, and arose, and was baptized.*

***"he is a chosen vessel unto me, to bear my name before the Gentiles, and kings, and the children of Israel"***—Paul/Saul/was one of two souls, chosen and given the power of the spirit of Jesus Christ.

## *Paul Was Also Benjamin (Son of Jacob) in Another Life*

According to Wikipedia **Benjamin** was the last-born of Jacob's 12 sons and the second and last son of Rachel. He was the founder of the Israelite Tribe of Benjamin. In the Biblical account, unlike Rachel's first son, Joseph, Benjamin was born in Canaan. He died in Egypt on the 11th of Marcheshvan, which was also his birthday, in 1443 BC at the age of 111. In the Qur'an, Benjamin is referred to as a righteous young child who remained with Jacob when the older brothers plotted against Joseph.

According to the Torah, Benjamin's name arose when Jacob deliberately corrupted the name *Benoni*, the original name of *Benjamin*, since *Benoni* was an allusion to Rachel's dying just after she had given birth, as it means *son of my pain*.

Jacob gave a blessing for his son Benjamin during Jacob's departure.

**Genesis 49:27 (KJV)**
*[27]Benjamin shall ravin as a wolf: in the morning he shall devour the prey, and at night he shall divide the spoil.*

**Wolves** are the essence of stamina, known to run 35 miles a day in pursuit of prey. They are highly misunderstood animals, who have gained the reputation of being cold blooded. In reality, wolves are friendly and social creatures. Aggression is something they avoid, preferring rather to growl or create a posture to show dominance.

Even though living in close-knit packs provides wolves with a strong sense of family, they are still able to maintain their individuality. Wolves represent the spirit of freedom, but they realize that having individual freedom requires having responsibilities.

Because the wolf as a symbol is a teacher and pathfinder, he comes when we need guidance in our lives. Those who have a wolf totem will move on to teach others about sacredness and spirituality. The wolf can also teach how to balance the responsibility of family needs and not to lose one's personal identity.

The wolf teaches us to develop strength and confidence in our decisions. He shows we will learn to trust our insights once we learn how to value our inner voice. This wisdom keeps us from inappropriate action.

Benjamin, who was also Paul/Saul in another life, has also reincarnated for this joyous occasion. He is a chosen vessel to bear the name of God in front of all the people and the children of Mother-Father-God. In this life Paul/Benjamin is a gifted healer and medium physic and a dear friend of mine. She was the first to give me a message from Arch Angel Michael that I would be writing a book about spirituality. A plan we made before incarnating in this life☺

## Chapter 999

# THE WORLD TO COME—OUR KINGDOM COME

### Elijah's Mission

*"At the appointed time, it is written, you are destined to calm the wrath of God before it breaks out in fury, to turn the hearts of parents to their children, and to restore the tribes of Jacob"* (**Ecclesiasticus 48:10**).

### *A Spiritual Point Where Reality Emerges*

**Revelation 14 (KJV)**
*¹And I looked, and, lo, a Lamb stood on the mount Zion, and with him an hundred forty and four thousand, having his Father's name written in their foreheads. ²And I heard a voice from heaven, as the voice of many waters, and as the voice of a great thunder: and I heard the voice of harpers harping with their harps:*

*³And they sung as it were a new song before the throne, and before the four beasts, and the elders: and no man could learn that song but the hundred and forty and four thousand, which were redeemed from the earth. ⁴These are they which were not defiled with women; for they are virgins. These are they which follow the Lamb whithersoever he goeth. These were redeemed from among men, being the first fruits unto God and to the Lamb.*

The first born were to God the Creator—the Lamb (Tribes of Jacob). All "lambs" referring to the pure divine blueprint. *⁵And in their mouth* was found no guile: for they are without fault before the throne of God.

⁶And I saw another angel fly in the midst of heaven, having the everlasting gospel to preach unto them that dwell on the earth, and to every nation, and kindred, and tongue, and people, ⁷Saying with a loud voice, Fear God, and give glory to him; for the hour of his judgment is come: and worship him that made heaven, and earth, and the sea, and the fountains of waters.

⁸And there followed another angel, saying, Babylon is fallen, is fallen, that great city, because she made all nations drink of the wine of the wrath of her fornication.

⁹And the third angel followed them, saying with a loud voice, If any man worship the beast and his image, and receive his mark in his forehead, or in his hand, ¹⁰The same shall drink of the wine of the wrath of God, which is poured out without mixture into the cup of his indignation; and he shall be tormented with fire and brimstone in the presence of the holy angels, and in the presence of the Lamb:

¹¹And the smoke of their torment ascendeth up for ever and ever: and they have no rest day nor night, who worship the beast and his image, and whosoever receiveth the mark of his name. ¹²Here is the patience of the saints: here are they that keep the commandments of God, and the faith of Jesus.

¹³And I heard a voice from heaven saying unto me, Write, Blessed are the dead which die in the Lord from henceforth: Yea, saith the Spirit, that they may rest from their labours; and their works do follow them. ¹⁴And I looked, and behold a white cloud, and upon the cloud one sat like unto the Son of man, having on his head a golden crown, and in his hand a sharp sickle.

¹⁵And another angel came out of the temple, crying with a loud voice to him that sat on the cloud, Thrust in thy sickle, and reap: for the time is come for thee to reap; for the harvest of the earth is ripe. ¹⁶And he

that sat on the cloud thrust in his sickle on the earth; and the earth was reaped.

[17]And another angel came out of the temple which is in heaven, he also having a sharp sickle. [18]And another angel came out from the altar, which had power over fire; and cried with a loud cry to him that had the sharp sickle, saying, Thrust in thy sharp sickle, and gather the clusters of the vine of the earth; for her grapes are fully ripe.

[19]And the angel thrust in his sickle into the earth, and gathered the vine of the earth, and cast it into the great winepress of the wrath of God. [20]And the winepress was trodden without the city, and blood came out of the winepress, even unto the horse bridles, by the space of a thousand and six hundred furlongs.

## Who Are The 144,000?

**Revelation 7:3-8 (KJV)**
[3]Saying, Hurt not the earth, neither the sea, nor the trees, till we have sealed the servants of our God in their foreheads. [4]And I heard the number of them which were sealed: and there were sealed an hundred and forty and four thousand of all the tribes of the children of Israel. [5]Of the tribe of Juda were sealed twelve thousand. Of the tribe of Reuben were sealed twelve thousand. Of the tribe of Gad were sealed twelve thousand. [6]Of the tribe of Aser were sealed twelve thousand. Of the tribe of Nephthalim were sealed twelve thousand. Of the tribe of Manasses were sealed twelve thousand. [7]Of the tribe of Simeon were sealed twelve thousand. Of the tribe of Levi were sealed twelve thousand. Of the tribe of Issachar were sealed twelve thousand. [8]Of the tribe of Zabulon were sealed twelve thousand. Of the tribe of Joseph were sealed twelve thousand. Of the tribe of Benjamin were sealed twelve thousand.

Do not harm the earth or the sea or the trees, until after we have sealed the servants of God on their foreheads. And I heard the number of the sealed, a hundred and forty-four thousand, sealed from every tribe of the sons of Israel:

The above paragraph translated is simply God's plan to protect his children. In order to protect us, God sealed our identity by hiding the tribes (our unused DNA) until a time when we have learned the lessons needed to transform into our spiritual bodies. Those who are not of the seed, those spirits who do not have the pureness of the lamb will never be able to raise their vibrations high enough to cause us any further harm.

The key ingredient we each were given is oil—our Free Will and Choice. Without this, others who were not of the lamb would have been able to slip in through the cracks and it would have been all for nothing.

We have all been in an institution "sealed" away from our truth, learning to be masters without having access to our gifts and abilities. Then we created a master plan together to be free from the old systems of living in a human body and returning once again to our divinity.

The light workers and world servers have broken through the seal as planned and these souls are now holding the door open, lighting and showing the way, helping the many others make the journey. Eventually, one by one, tribe by tribe until all 12 tribes/sons of Jacob will all make it home again. Our soul's purpose is BRINGING JACOB HOME AGAIN!

**Revelation 13:16-17 (KJV)**
*[16]And he causeth all, both small and great, rich and poor, free and bond, to receive a mark in their right hand, or in their foreheads: [17]And that no man might buy or sell, save he that had the mark, or the name of the beast, or the number of his name*

The seal on the forehead is the identification of one of God's children—a mark that cannot be bought, sold, stolen, or reproduced in any way shape of form. Do you understand the mysteries of the Universe have been under lock and key so that they do not get into the wrong hands again? It has taken many lifetimes for "olive" our souls to go around the track over and over again until there would be enough souls to break away from the darkness into the light.

**Acts 1 (KJV)**
¹²Then returned they unto Jerusalem from the mount called Olivet, which is from Jerusalem a Sabbath day's journey.

The Mount of Olives, also known as Mount Olivet, is a mountain ridge east of Jerusalems's Old City in East Jerusalem. Jesus gave an end-time prophecy at this location.

## Clearing The Hay

Back in the days of Lemuria and Atlantis, the secrets of the Universe got into the wrong hands and this was cause for our demise.

If you want the keys to gain entry to the knowledge of the other elements, you will first need to "clear the hay". Throughout our lifetimes, we have come to gain knowledge (light and information). The lessons we each learn bring out the best and worst in us (our personality). When we incarnate into the next life, we bring that personality with us—it is part of us. Each lifetime with our soul families we have created and orchestrated the experiences, possibilities and probabilities that we felt would accomplish the life purposes required for each individually and collectively.

It is extremely important that we understand and come to terms with those individuals who we feel have caused us pain and sorrow. These souls have agreed in advance of their incarnation to provide us with these lessons, therefore helping YOU expand your consciousness enough to break free and find home. Forgive all and be very grateful for these souls—it is this kind of **UNCONDITIONAL LOVE** that conquers all.

This plan was created based on our life reviews each time we leave our physical bodies. The plan includes what we did—what went right, what went wrong, and what we could have done better to get the job done so that the next time we return we can come back greater than the time before. OH YAH! It's just like a business plan and we are all in it to win it together in "oneness"!

As the veil has been thinning over the years, some of us have been able to pierce through the density of the Earth that resides in the third-dimensional energy. The Earth has also been freed, leaving the old Earth behind for those who haven't made it out yet! Many of the light workers who incarnated into this time in history and the Earth have now entered the higher frequencies that are required to complete a spiritual transformation. Think of it as finding the keys that unlock the door to enter a new house, a better house, a house filled with unconditional love, gifts and abilities, treasures so great, our imagination cannot comprehend!

## *The Tribes of Israel—Sons of Jacob*

12,000 from the tribe of Judah
12,000 from the tribe of Reuben
12,000 from the tribe of Gad
12,000 from the tribe of Asher
12,000 from the tribe of Naphtali
12,000 from the tribe of Manasseh
12,000 from the tribe of Simeon
12,000 from the tribe of Levi
12,000 from the tribe of Issachar
12,000 from the tribe of Zebulun
12,000 from the tribe of Joseph
12,000 from the tribe of Benjamin

**Revelation 14:1 (KJV)**
*[1]And I looked, and, lo, a Lamb stood on the mount Sion, and with him an hundred forty and four thousand, having his Father's name written in their foreheads*

*Then I looked, and behold, on mount Zion* (a spiritual point where reality emerges) *stood the Lamb* (the pure one), *and with him 144,000 who had his name and his Father's name written on their foreheads.*

Note: 144,000 = 144 Blueprints + 000 infinite number of infinite spiritual beings

**Revelation 14:3-5 (KJV)**
*³And they sung as it were a new song before the throne, and before the four beasts, and the elders: and no man could learn that song but the hundred and forty and four thousand, which were redeemed from the earth. ⁴These are they which were not defiled with women; for they are virgins. These are they which follow the Lamb whithersoever he goeth. These were redeemed from among men, being the first fruits unto God and to the Lamb. ⁵And in their mouth was found no guile: for they are without fault before the throne of God.*

Mount Zion is the spiritual point from where reality emerges.

Each of the 12 Tribes (12 sons of Jacob) has 12 Blueprints making up the 144 Blueprints. Every spiritual being, including every man, woman and child, angels, and ascended masters who are of the lamb, are among the 144,000 represented.

God our Creator leaves no one behind—he loves all of his children. He knows all of his children by the pureness of the heart—their soul song or signature that shows the light. All spirits of God the Creator have pure hearts (pure like a lamb).

When we are in our spirit form, we know this. When we incarnate into a physical body, we are pure like lambs. The second we are born into a physical body, we are still pure but we have been covered up from part of the DNA blueprint and, therefore, we cannot remember our divine spirits. Our spiritual beings are invisible and we go through life unaware of the truths about who we are and not knowing how to connect to the other tribes.

This separation from our blueprint, our birthrights, is part of the divine grand master plan created by our God the Creator so that we could find our way home—all of us—one by one and all together united as ONE without contaminating the pure seeds! By experiencing and learning the lessons as a spiritual being having human experiences, we are able to find our way home as well as help others who are on our path.

Many of the experiences created much pain and suffering for humanity. We must love those who created this for us—it is their sacrifice to help you learn the lesson. They are your soul family and you have done this for them in other lifetimes as well.

Many have left the Earth before the "SHIFT" of consciousness, the Christ's consciousness, and will return in another lifetime if they choose. Many will return to the old Earth; some will complete their spiritual transformation at that time and it will be easier due to the new knowledge and the new energies now available to make it possible. It will take some time to get all of us back together again, therefore, some had to stay back to hold the old system in place until we all get through the door.

This is the time of the New Earth and the New Human because we have evolved into a higher dimension—a higher frequency that allows us to bring Jacob home, to become one again with our spirits. Do not judge those who choose to stay in the old system—there is a reason for everything. We can guide but we cannot do the lessons for others. We have an individual commitment to unite as ONE!

The belief of recognizing the spiritual self, one's own psychological and karma battles and how to overcome them, and eventual ascension—a spiritual transformation of releasing and letting go, a "clearing of the hay", burning away the debris that covers and blocks our pure divine hearts. "The Kingdom of Heaven within The Holy Book of The Great Invisible Spirit☺" has been created to assist those who are ready and have enough "oil" to move forward.

## *Chapter IV*

# THE SOUL KNOWS

### *Your Soul Family*

These souls can be your children, grandchildren, your best friend, husband, wife, worst enemy, boss, business partner, sister, brother, niece, nephew, any number of possibilities, and even the school teacher that encouraged you with patience and kindness, or the school teacher that discouraged you with impatience and cruelty. However, as you, the personality has free will, so you may create a path that takes you in a different direction, and this is why you have to make possible agreements with so many.

A soul family will work together for many, many lifetimes. Some members of your soul family who do not reincarnate at the same time stay in spirit form during your physical existence for the ones who have reincarnated—the family working on the other side of the veil to help and guide their family on this side.

They can visit you in dreams, inspire you with thoughts and ideas, or in some cases, speak to you directly. ☺ You will start to see them with different eyes and hear them with different ears and feel them around and within.

As you reincarnate into each lifetime, you make agreements and contracts with many different souls. We all have our own **"karma"** to work out. We are all helping each other while helping ourselves.

## *Karma*

**Karma** is known as "the law of cause and effect" and plays a central role in determining how one's life should be lived. Spirits are encouraged to choose how (and when) to suffer retribution for the wrong they did in previous lives. Disabilities, physical or mental impairment, or even an unlucky life are due to the choices a spirit makes before reincarnating (that is, before being born to a new life).

The choice of a life of hardships is a way to learn and know what joy and happiness is. We must experience both the negative and positive in our lives to bring balance to our soul and the souls of others. The choices we make influence many other souls who also need to experience certain events in their life.

The time is here to change the game—create a new way of life. We don't have to complete our karma anymore to create the balance in our soul. We can let go of present and past life baggage and move into our spiritual presence of being without leaving our physical bodies. There is much work to do for anyone who is willing and ready to move up the ladder to the Kingdom of Heaven right here on the "New Earth".

Karma is not fate, for humans act with free will creating experiences and fulfilling lifetime and soul purposes. If one sows goodness, one will reap goodness; if one sows evil, one will reap evil. Your thoughts become things. What you project into the Universe will return to you like looking through a mirror.

Karma refers to the totality of our actions and their connected reactions in this and previous lives, all of which has determined our future.

**Karmic clearing** can uplift and awaken you physically, emotionally, mentally and spiritually. It will clear the blocks from lifetimes associated with the "karma" you are trying to clear that may be preventing you from gaining the best of your potential in this life or from achieving total well-being through peace of heart and mind. You can also clear "karma" between you and other souls.

Karmic clearing happens on a multi-dimensional level, as you are a multidimensional being. When you clear the debris, burn the stubble, clear the hay, you will clear it on all levels of your multidimensional being.

**Proverbs 27:19**
*"As in water face answereth to face, so the heart of man to man.*

## Working Out Your Karma

If you were an assassin in another life, you might choose enduring cancer of the esophagus in this life. Or perhaps you were a slave in another life and you have carried forward the negative karma of having low self-esteem. If you have "karma" to fulfill, you set up your life plan with a set of possibilities and probabilities that will most likely take place for you to complete the lesson you wish to learn. It is important to note that these lessons, as you are very well aware, are not always pretty. If you set up a plan to learn a certain lesson and you do not achieve it in this lifetime, you will try it again in your next reincarnation. The next time you return, you may choose different sets of possibilities and probabilities in order to create the experience you are trying to have.

When the spirit leaves the body and crosses over, the soul is given a life review of your entire life—lessons learned, what you could have done differently, what worked, what didn't work. There is absolutely no judgment there.

## Suffering Brought Him Great Joy

Not quite two years ago, a member of my soul family came into my life for a brief encounter that was planned long before either of us had incarnated into this life. Some people will come into your life for a lifetime and others will come into your life for only 30 minutes. There is a reason for everything—every single second of your life!

I was called upon to provide healing for a young man suffering from cancer of the esophagus (unknown to me until after the healing session—I knew he had cancer but I did not know where the cancer was in his system). His family was told that there was nothing more they could do for him.

Just as I arrived in the hospital room where he was being cared for by his mother, he was not responding well to the food they were trying to feed him. I suggested I wait in the waiting room (steps away) until he was settled. I remember how difficult it was for me at that very moment in time. I was very emotional. I remember thinking it was a good thing that I had this time alone before I met him until I was settled. Even though I had never met him before, I was overwhelmed with feeling like he was one of my own and such knowing I can't imagine for anyone; I can't imagine myself as a parent watching this happen to my child. I knew right then that this was by far the most difficult moment I had ever encountered at that time and that I had to overcome this emotion immediately in order to step into my work. I felt deep sympathy, compassion and sadness. I went deep into myself to find that place where I could detach myself from him, his illness and my feelings. I had to go within and find that place and find it fast. I needed courage and strength and I went deep within to get it, asking spirit and God the creator for assistance.

Minutes later, his mother came into the waiting area to inform me that he had settled enough—she began to tell me more about his illness and how this was not suppose to be happening to him. I explained briefly details about the healing. I explained that I do not decide what healing will take place, but certainly that a healing of some kind would in fact take place—one that is appropriate for him at this time. I explained the healing process of accessing frequencies (light and information) through a higher level of consciousness. I explained that we each have the universal rights to the law of free will and choice. Each soul is free to choose however we wish. I explained how the healing is a balance of the physical, mental, emotional and spiritual bodies, which means whatever balance is received will stay with us in spirit form and physical form—both if we chose to stay.

During the session, I felt the frequencies around the back of his neck and around his stomach. He didn't seem to have any registers that I could see—however, he looked very restful and at peace. Upon completion, I touched his shoulder ever so softly as I told him I would when it was complete. I told him not to speak and stay resting while his healing continued into the night.

As I was leaving his bedside, he turned to look at me—I saw his soul and felt the warmth of his spirit thanking me. I wasn't sure at this moment what it all meant, but it felt appropriate. It felt serene. It felt like you would feel if you had a chronic back pain and now it was gone and you wanted to acknowledge that and words were not necessary. It felt like joy, love and happiness without the physical expression of it. It felt soft and satisfied.

It was his soul choice to experience cancer of the esophagus. In a past life, he was an assassin and he slit the throats of others. All of us have experienced situations in one or more lifetimes that upon our departure we have reviewed the results of, our feelings and several other variables. It is then we can create a new experience to offset the experience, bringing a balancing to our karma.

He received a healing out of the darkness into the light, creating a soulful feeling of light and love. In a previous incarnation, he had deep-seeded guilt and the healing gave him peace and a knowing at the soul level. The soul creates new experiences to create a balance, a physiological positioning, the lessening of discomfort and pain.

Even though it was his suffering, it was with great joy that he completed this part of his choices. He was not consciously aware of this as he was going through this particular lifetime experience—however, unconsciously he was fully aware—*the soul knows.*

There are no words to describe the feeling I got, the sense of *knowing* that the soul was thanking and appreciating my being. It was at a very deep level and it was beautiful. And, at the same time, my soul knew it had completed a karmic choice by stepping through that door providing the healing and allowing my spirit to be the light. It was a major turning point in this life.

The details of our life are skillfully and masterfully planned out by ourselves, our soul self and our soul families. This example alone was carefully planned out with his own soul and many, many others to balance that one experience that had effects on not just the two of us but many of his family, friends and other acquaintances in that lifetime and other lifetimes.

That particular life experience was divinely orchestrated and, for me, I would see the treasure on my path, pick it up, and continue my journey down my path in this lifetime—stepping into the unknown, fearless so that I could step yet onto a larger stage where many others would benefit. In exchange, I was able to provide him with a balance of his spiritual body, assisting in his spiritual transformation to the other side.

Throughout your spiritual transformation—to the Kingdom of Heaven within the Holy Book of the Great Invisible Spirit☺, you no longer will need to leave your body to complete your karma. You will be reconnected to your full spiritual being, which has been disconnected for eons. You will become aware of and have access to your unique gifts and abilities—something your soul has always known. NOW, for the very first time ever, we can change our DNA! Did you hear me?

## *I Could Not See—I Could Not Hear*

My dear friend Donna, my soul sister, passed away so young and so not ready to leave her family and friends and they were not ready for her to go. She is a very joyful and fun loving spirit who will return to work with me again. Her life experiences while she was here affected many souls, including mine. She lived a rich and endearing life, having an abundance of life experiences to take with her—some stinky roses and some pretty nice smelling skunks.

I was taking a nice leisure nature walk one day and while I was walking I asked my dear friend, who is so close yet so far away because of the veil that makes her spirit invisible, I asked when she would be ready to start working with me again. It had been at least a year since she passed but I had not received any confirmation of her being around like I had with the others. I asked her if she was still resting and would it be long before I would hear from her? I let her know that I could really use some help from her in preparation of writing this book. Here is what she said:

*"My eyes were open but I could not see, my ears were listening and I could not hear, my heart was closed—I could not feel 'ALL THAT IS.'"*

Thank you, my dear beloved friend, for your inspiring words sent from the other side. You are a beautiful, loving, and powerful spiritual being. Things have changed and YES, we can get there from here now. ☺ Love & Light

You have created a plan with many other souls. Like me, you are here with other soul family members who were on Earth in previous lifetimes. I have located several souls, some of whom are close *family* in this life; some who are close *friends* in this life; and then some who I am meeting in this life for the very first time. Many of them have been here with me during one or more major historical events.

You will start to notice if you haven't already, new people coming into your life right now. The same is also happening with people leaving your life—some who have made the choice not to be here during "The Shift" on this planet possibly for a higher calling or perhaps souls moving in another direction—divinely guided by their own angels. It is a sad and sorrowful time when our loved ones chose to depart. It is never easy—it really hurts when you lose someone close to you. You need to **know** they are right there the minute you think their name, they are always coming to watch over you—we are all multidimensional beings.

I realize as I write this that this is really hard for many to accept because it is not what you have known. It will take some time to understand and become in tune with it. I can tell you the feeling of being connected to a loved one who has crossed over is a gift from GOD! It is the most amazing, wonderful feeling when you can feel the touch of their hands on your skin. A spiritual transformation—it's a new day, a new dawning, and we no longer have to suffer the pain of losing a loved one because they are no longer lost or separated; they have always been there and will always be.

# Chapter V

# THE NEW AGE—THE GOLDEN AGE

It is the coming of the New Age, The Golden Age, The Age of Aquarius. Most have counted down the years, the months and the days to see what exactly would happen December 21, 2012. The world and the son of man are ending old beliefs and old ways and for the very first time ever, man will not have to start over. Together we have created the "New Earth" where we will no longer live in dense energy keeping us separated from our true identities. It is a time of celebration!

## *Energetic Signature—Coat of Many Colours*

I had just learned I was a teacher, a midwife and a doctor of bones in more recent previous lives, just to mention a few. The fact that my mother in this life had spent her entire life in and out of orthopedic surgeon offices due to her crippling arthritis disease had my undivided attention. Not a coincidence—there are no coincidences and, may I remind you once again, there is a reason for everything. ☺

My new-found identity literally smacked me right in the face—a feeling I cannot describe. At the time, I was dumbfounded by my *knowing* of what I had found and I couldn't comprehend how I knew it, as I stared at the picture of my spirit in another suit! Once I started to write down my experiences in this life, it became crystal clear that there had always been a plan—a divinely guided plan. The nudges once soft and gentle started to appear in bright, colorful lights!

The Kingdom of Heaven within The Holy Book of the Great Invisible Spirit ☺

We each have our own unique, energetic signature, a soul song—or I call it our "coat of many colors". ☺ SPIRIT is guiding our way and we with our oil (our will)—"free will and choice"—have happily accepted the honor of playing out our parts on the grandest stage of all. We have agreed and now our spiritual beings are here in the physical on this Earth plane for the most amazing time in history. There is a reason why you are here for this special time.

For me, my part is to deliver this message—a message I have delivered many times before, but only this time the energy is available to bring the information matching the vibration of the masses of people who are ready to receive it. This time the radio signal is invented (available) for all to hear.

Connecticut, like most places on the planet, is not the easiest place to get to know people especially in the age of cyberspace when everyone has a physical body but they don't seem to be present. ☺ I tried to make friends in everyday life experiences such as grocery shopping, walking, bowling and volunteering for the Red Cross.

I remember one of my first encounters at the local grocery store in Connecticut. I walked into the store looking straight ahead, smiling and saying hello to everyone as I passed by when a woman ran right into my grocery cart. This was not a really big deal as this happens often and then I was about to say, "Oh, don't worry about it," but she didn't even look at me or apologize. It was like I was not there; or maybe she was somewhere else or vice versa? I was dumbfounded as I watched her move about the store as if no one else existed. For a minute, I thought it was a "Stepford wife" encounter or maybe I was in a dream.

Recently, I had one of those dreams where I know I was actually there. You KNOW the kind—the dream that feels so real. In this dream, I was in a huge hallway at a hospital. There were several people in the hall walking, sitting, standing, and lying down. I was with a young girl who was in her 20s. The girl was ill with cancer and I told her I would like to help her and give her a healing. After explaining to her what the healing was about, she laid down on the cot with her blanket to receive the healing. I tried to stand beside her on the cot and make my way around it. I was struggling with people coming and going and at one point a woman came in holding a child in a car seat. The woman put the car seat right down tight up to the cot where I was trying to stand. Again, it was like I didn't exist—in fact, I didn't exist in her reality.

It's complicated when you leave your reality to assist someone in another AND then someone else appears who seems to be yet in another! More about this in the next book called "Invisible to Visible: Beyond the Veil" which I co-wrote with Vanessa.

It was a dream—at night we travel and when we remember, we call them dreams. In this dream, I travelled to help someone in another dimension that really exists. When we see a ghost, they are not always aware that we see them. They are souls who haven't passed over to the light. They are wandering around the Earth. Sometimes they see us and we don't see them. Other times, we see them and they don't see us.

Some people have the ability to see ghosts and some people have the ability to see spirits who have crossed over to the light. Then there are others who have the ability to see angels and guides. They usually have the extra gift of communicating with them as well.

There are aspects of you in other lifetimes, and there are aspects of you in other dimensions of parallel existences—you exist on many levels past, present and future. It is fascinating and magnificent and yet right now so very mind boggling to comprehend all of this at this time.

I have been very fortunate to experience many dreams. Some dreams, I remember bits and pieces and other dreams I remember vividly. Some of those vivid dreams have been significant markers on my path.☺

## God Will Increase

Joseph means "God will increase".

**Genesis 30:23-25 (KJV)**
*²³And she conceived, and bare a son; and said, God hath taken away my reproach: ²⁴And she called his name Joseph; and said, The LORD shall add to me another son. ²⁵And it came to pass, when Rachel had born Joseph, that Jacob said unto Laban, Send me away, that I may go unto mine own place, and to my country.*

According to Wikipedia Joseph's half brothers hated him so much, especially for his dreams. Joseph, son of Israel (Jacob) and Rachel lived in the land of Canaan with 11 brothers and one sister. He was Rachel's firstborn and Israel's 11th son. Of all the sons, it was believed that Joseph was loved by his father the most. It has also been believed that Israel gave his son Joseph a "long coat of many colors". Israel's favoritism toward Joseph caused his half brothers to hate him, and when Joseph was 17 years old, he had two dreams that made his brothers plot his journey.

In the first dream, Joseph and his brothers gathered bundles of grain (or as I would say perhaps to create manna?) Then all of the grain bundles that had been prepared by the brothers gathered around Joseph's bundle and bowed down to it. In the second dream, the sun (father), the moon (mother) and 11 stars (brothers) bowed down to Joseph himself. When he told these two dreams to his brothers, they despised him for the implications that the family would be bowing down to Joseph. They became jealous that their father would even ponder over Joseph's words concerning these dreams (***Genesis 37:1-11***).

## Spirit Dreams

### The Time Is Nigh

When I was a young teenager, I remember one of those vivid dreams where I was flying around the house in my nightgown. I flew three times around before returning to bed. My spiritual self was ready for flight, but the soul knew it was not yet time. Apparently, that was a practice run. ☺

## Messages From The Other Side

I have had several dreams visiting my dear beloved sister-in-law who was giving me messages from the other side. I remember telling the entire family about the dreams as I was interpreting the meaning each time she came to me. She was angelic—she smiled and had no words. She showed me by creating a scene with a story where I could hear myself but I could not hear her—but yet I knew what she was saying.

## A Spirit In Flight

I was in a park. The high top was snowy with many trees. There were people running around "to and fro"—probably looking for "grain and oil" to make "manna".☺ There was a trail that went down to a bright, sunshiny, sandy beach along a big, blue body of water. And on the beach there was a bald EAGLE much bigger than me—in fact, it was like we traded our size.

The EAGLE crouched down so that I could get on his back and he flew up and away soaring over the water, the valleys, the mountaintops and the hills. It was an amazing trip to see everything from up so high. I remember I didn't want to go back down. Then the EAGLE gently flew back down, crouched down to let me off. I thanked him and he flew off.

To be able to have a view, to see and hear with a new set of eyes—eagle eyes—sight and sound in flight allowing information and light to come to you from a higher perspective is truly a gift of another kind. Dreams are insights, preparations and trainings for things to come.

## *Joseph the Light Worker*

Joseph's God-spark evolved into the Golden Age, a spirit filled with compassion and unconditional love. He endured life experiences both good and bad, allowing his energetic soul signature to increase and showing others the way with his light on the path through the door. Experiencing the hatred he received from his half brothers, being sold to slavery and then enduring a prison life are the experiences he created with other souls like his brothers before reincarnating into that life. The experiences mirror his guided message, which is the same message he brings into all of his lives during major historical events.

Like an eagle, Joseph could see, hear and feel "all that is" from a higher perspective. Although not an easy task, he was able to stay true to his identity by rising above all of life's trials and tribulations. No matter what was done to him, he never showed remorse or revenge, speaking only the truth.

Joseph's message can be interpreted by reviewing his life experiences just the same way Joseph and his soul family reviewed his life experiences once he completed his mission in that life. His message was received by the people who were seeking help in that time in history. The king was ready to know more about his own dreams and allowed himself to give and receive by using a much brighter light.

Joseph was the 11th son—firstborn of two sons born to Rachel and Jacob. Joseph was hated by the half brothers and abolished or separated from the family (separated from the sons (tribes) of Jacob). Joseph was then sold to slavery and ended up in prison, probably because of his gifts and abilities. His life was desolate and lonely, which opened a doorway to creating manna with his oil and grain.

He had dreams that came from within—he remained open to receive the information that he was given. Joseph was a light worker sharing his dreams and the information that helped him and many others including you.

Joseph was released from prison for the same reason he was put in prison, because he stayed true to his knowing and let go of any fear, judgment, worry or doubt that hold all of us hostage. While he had a growing, colorful aura (energetic signature) that he brought with him from lifetime to lifetime, he was able to locate the **keys** that would set him free to living a life of abundance, but he didn't do it for money.

**Joseph** "May Yahweh add" is an important character in the Hebrew Bible, where he connects the story of Abraham, Isaac and Jacob in Canaan to the subsequent story of the liberation of the Israelites from slavery in Egypt.

The time is now to be liberated from slavery and brought out of the ancient kingdom, and to become free to live a joyous, abundant life on the new Earth in the new kingdom—the Kingdom of Heaven within The Holy Book of The Great Invisible Spirit. ☺ It is time to reunite with your families and come out of the old, dark systems into the new light and new energy.

The Book of Genesis tells how Joseph was the 11th of Jacob's 12 sons and Rachel's firstborn. Joseph was sold into slavery by his jealous brothers, yet rose to become the most powerful man in Egypt next to the Pharaoh. When famine struck the land, he brought the sons of Israel down to Egypt, where they were settled in the Land of Goshen.

Joseph's experiences in the end created opportunity for all of his family.

**Genesis 37**
*[1]And Jacob dwelt in the land wherein his father was a stranger, in the land of Canaan. [2]These are the generations of Jacob. Joseph, being seventeen years old, was feeding the flock with his brethren; and the lad was with the sons of Bilhah, and with the sons of Zilpah, his father's wives: and Joseph brought unto his father their evil report. [3]Now Israel loved Joseph more than all his children, because he was the son of his old age: and he made him a **coat of many colors**.*

There is nothing "paranormal" in the Universe, except our limited understanding of Nature. What we think we *"know"* on Earth now is just a tiny drop in the dimensions of knowledge. In the distant past, people admired things they could not explain and called them "miracles". Long ago, people were able to see auras.

Advanced spiritual people such as Buddha, Christ and their immediate students were painted with golden halos around their heads because some artists could actually see auras. In Australia's remote West Kimberleys, you can find prehistoric cave paintings many thousands of years old depicting people with golden halos.

Everything in the Universe is a vibration. Every atom, every part of an atom, every electron, every elementary "particle", even our thoughts and consciousness are vibrations.

The aura is the electromagnetic field (EMF) that surrounds the human body and every organism and object in the galaxy.

The human energy field is a collection of electromagnetic energies of varying densities that infuse through and exit out from the physical body of a living person. These particles of energy are suspended around the human body in an oval-shaped field. This "auric egg" releases out from the body approximately 2-3 feet (1 meter on average) on all sides. It extends above the head and below the feet into the ground.

What did Joseph's brothers see? When they dumped him in the ditch, they thought they were taking away his coat of many colors. Nobody can take away your soul signature. It can be dimmed or brightened, but never taken away. Your light grows as your spirit grows—each soul has a unique energetic signature or soul song coded with color and sound.

**Genesis 37 (KJV)**
*⁴And when his brethren **saw that their father loved him more** than all his brethren, they hated him, and could not speak peaceably unto him. ⁵And Joseph dreamed a dream, and he told it his brethren: and they hated him yet the more. ⁶And he said unto them, Hear, I pray*

*you, this dream which I have dreamed:* ⁷*For, behold, we were binding sheaves in the field, and, lo, my sheaf arose, and also stood upright; and, behold, your sheaves stood round about, and made obeisance to my sheaf.* ⁸*And his brethren said to him, Shalt thou indeed reign over us? or shalt thou indeed have dominion over us? And they hated him yet the more for his dreams, and for his words.* ⁹*And he dreamed yet another dream, and told it his brethren, and said, Behold, I have dreamed a dream more; and, behold, the sun and the moon and the eleven stars made obeisance to me.* ¹⁰*And he told it to his father, and to his brethren: and his father rebuked him, and said unto him, What is this dream that thou hast dreamed? Shall I and thy mother and thy brethren indeed come to bow down ourselves to thee to the earth?* ¹¹*And his brethren envied him; but his father observed the saying.* ¹²*And his brethren went to feed their father's flock in Shechem.* ¹³*And Israel said unto Joseph, Do not thy brethren feed the flock in Shechem? come, and I will send thee unto them. And he said to him, Here am I.* ¹⁴*And he said to him, Go, I pray thee, see whether it be well with thy brethren, and well with the flocks; and bring me word again. So he sent him out of the vale of Hebron, and he came to Shechem.*

¹⁵*And a certain man found him, and, behold,* **he was wandering in the field**: *and the man asked him, saying, What seekest thou?* ¹⁶*And he said, I seek my brethren: tell me, I pray thee, where they feed their flocks.* ¹⁷*And the man said, They are departed hence; for I heard them say, Let us go to Dothan. And Joseph went after his brethren, and found them in Dothan.*

**"Wandering in the field"—quantum field, spiritual field (meditating)**

¹⁸*And when they saw him afar off, even before he came near unto them, they conspired against him to slay him.* ¹⁹*And they said one to another, Behold, this dreamer cometh.* ²⁰*Come now therefore, and let us slay him, and cast him into some pit, and we will say, Some evil beast hath devoured him: and we shall see what will become of his dreams.* ²¹*And Reuben heard it, and he delivered him out of their hands; and said, Let us not kill him.* ²²*And Reuben said unto them, Shed no blood, but cast him into this pit that is in the wilderness, and lay no hand upon*

him; that he might rid him out of their hands, to deliver him to his father again.

²³And it came to pass, when Joseph was come unto his brethren, that **they stript Joseph out of his coat, his coat of many colours that was on him;** ²⁴And they took him, and cast him into a pit: and the pit was empty, there was no water in it. ²⁵And they sat down to eat **bread**: and they lifted up their eyes and looked, and, behold, a company of Ishmeelites came from Gilead with their camels bearing spicery and balm and myrrh, going to carry it down to Egypt. ²⁶And Judah said unto his brethren, what profit is it if we slay our brother, and conceal his blood? ²⁷Come, and let us sell him to the Ishmeelites, and let not our hand be upon him; for he is our brother and our flesh. And his brethren were content.

²⁸Then there passed by Midianites merchantmen; and they drew and lifted up Joseph out of the pit, and sold Joseph to the Ishmeelites for twenty pieces of silver: and they brought Joseph into Egypt. ²⁹And Reuben returned unto the pit; and, behold, Joseph was not in the pit; and he rent his clothes. ³⁰And he returned unto his brethren, and said, The child is not; and I, whither shall I go? ³¹And they took Joseph's coat, and killed a kid of the goats, and dipped the coat in the blood; ³²And they sent the coat of many colours, and they brought it to their father; and said, This have we found: know now whether it be thy son's coat or no. ³³And he knew it, and said, It is my son's coat; an evil beast hath devoured him; Joseph is without doubt rent in pieces. ³⁴And Jacob rent his clothes, and put sackcloth upon his loins, and mourned for his son many days. ³⁵And all his sons and all his daughters rose up to comfort him; but he refused to be comforted; and he said, For I will go down into the grave unto my son mourning. Thus his father wept for him. ³⁶And the Midianites sold him into Egypt unto Potiphar, an officer of Pharaoh's, and captain of the guard.

## Angels Among Us

Wikipedia also states the warden put Joseph in charge of the other prisoners, and soon afterward Pharaoh's chief cup bearer and chief baker, who had offended the Pharaoh, were thrown into the prison. They both had dreams, and they asked Joseph to help interpret them. The chief cup bearer had held a vine in his hand with three branches that brought forth grapes; he took them to Pharoah and put them in his cup. The chief baker had three baskets of bread on his head, intended for Pharoah, but some birds came along and ate the bread. Joseph told them that within three days, the chief cup bearer would be reinstated, but the chief baker would be hanged. Joseph requested the cup bearer to mention him to Pharaoh and secure his release from prison, but the cup bearer, reinstalled in office, forgot Joseph.

After Joseph was in prison for two more years, Pharaoh had two dreams that disturbed him. He dreamt of seven lean cows that rose out of the river and devoured seven fat cows; and, of seven withered ears of grain that devoured seven fat ears. Pharaoh's wise men were unable to interpret these dreams, but the chief cup bearer remembered Joseph and spoke of his skill to Pharaoh. Joseph was called for and interpreted the dreams as foretelling that seven years of abundance would be followed by seven years of famine, and advised Pharaoh to store surplus grain during the years of abundance.

## Vizier of Egypt

Pharaoh acknowledged that Joseph's proposal to store grain during the abundant period was very wise. So before Joseph was even 30 years old, Pharaoh released him from prison and put him in charge over "all the land of Egypt" as Vizier. The Pharaoh took off his signet ring and put it on Joseph's hand, then clothed him in fine linen and put a gold necklace around his neck. He was then renamed Zaphnath-Paaneah and was given Asenath, the daughter of Potipherah who was the priest of ON, to be his wife.

Remember the "Widow from Zarapath" who had a little flour (grain or manna) and oil (O-WILL)—she had just enough for her and her son Jonah for their last supper and then when Elijah showed up she took a chance into the unknown because something within her knew and so she made a feast (manifested), a meal for Elijah who performed a miracle of having a continuous flow of manna and oil that would keep them alive throughout the three and half years (the years of tribulation). There seems to be a pattern of the same message given here.

During those seven years of abundance, Joseph ensured that the storehouses were full and that all produce was measured until there was so much that it became immeasurable. In the final year of abundance, **Asenath bore two children to Joseph: Manasseh and Ephraim.** When the famine came, it was so severe that people from surrounding nations "from all over the Earth" came to Egypt to buy **bread** as this nation was the only kingdom prepared for the seven-year drought. The narrative also indicates that they went straight to Joseph or were directed to him, even by Pharaoh himself, so as to buy from him (***Genesis 41:37-57***).

Joseph was a spiritual interpreter.

The seven-year famine became so severe that toward the later period, even Egypt was being strangled. Because the Egyptians had used up all of their money to buy grain in the previous years, there was no more money left. All they had was their livestock and even that dwindled down to nothing. As a last resort, all of the inhabitants of Egypt, less the Egyptian priestly class, sold all of their properties to Joseph for seed. These properties now became the property of the Pharaoh, or in other words, government property.

Joseph also set a mandate that because they would be harvesting seed on government property, a fifth of the produce should go to the Pharaoh. A fifth to the Pharaoh continued down as well to at least the days of Moses (Genesis 47:20-31).

## Brothers Sent to the Old Kingdom—Egypt

According to Wikipedia, in the second year of famine, Joseph's half brothers were sent to Egypt by their father Israel to buy goods. When they came to Egypt, they stood before the Vizier but did not recognize him to be their brother Joseph. However, Joseph *did* recognize them and did not receive them kindly; rather he disguised himself and spoke to them in the Egyptian language using an interpreter.

He did not speak at all to them in his native tongue, Hebrew. After questioning them as to where they came from, he accused them of being spies. They pleaded with him that their only purpose was to buy grain for their family in the land of Canaan. After they mentioned that they had left a younger brother at home, the Vizier (Joseph) demanded that he be brought to Egypt as a demonstration of their veracity. This brother was Joseph's blood brother, Benjamin.

He placed his brothers in prison for **three** days. On the third day, he brought them out of prison to reiterate that he wanted their youngest brother brought to Egypt to demonstrate their veracity. The brothers conferred amongst themselves, speaking in Hebrew, reflecting on the wrong they had done to Joseph.

Joseph understood what they were saying and removed himself from their presence because he was caught in emotion. When he returned, the Vizier took Simeon and bound him as a hostage. Then he had their donkeys prepared with grain and sent the other brothers back to Canaan. Unbeknownst to them, Joseph had also returned their money to their money sacks (***Genesis 42:1-28***).

## The Silver Lining

The remaining brothers returned to their father in Canaan and told him all that had transpired in Egypt. They also discovered that all of their money sacks still had money in them and they were dismayed. Then they informed their father that the Vizier demanded that Benjamin be brought before him to demonstrate that they were honest men.

Israel became greatly distressed, feeling that they treated him badly. After they had consumed all of the grain that they brought back from Egypt, Israel told his sons to go back to Egypt for more grain.

With Reuben and Judah's persistence, they persuaded their father to let Benjamin join them for fear of Egyptian retribution (***Genesis 42:29-43:15***).

Upon their return to Egypt, the brothers were received by the steward of the house of Joseph. When they were brought to Joseph's house, they became afraid because of the returned money in their money sacks. They thought that the missed transaction would somehow be used against them as way to induct them as slaves and confiscate their possessions.

So they immediately informed the steward of what had transpired to get a feel of the situation. On the contrary, the Steward put them at ease, telling them not to worry of the money, and then he brought out their brother Simeon. They all went into the house of Joseph and were received with hospitality. When the Vizier (Joseph) appeared, they gave him gifts from their father.

Joseph saw and inquired of Benjamin and was overcome by emotion, but did not show it. He retreated to his chambers and wept. When he gained control of himself, he returned and brought out the feast. Now as it was at that time, Egyptians did not allow Hebrews to eat with them at the same table, as that was considered loathsome. So when the Vizier (Joseph) brought food over to the table of the sons of Israel, they were astonished (***Genesis 43:16-44:34***).

That night, Joseph ordered his steward to load the brother's donkeys with food and all their money. The money they brought was double what they had from the first trip. Deceptively, Joseph also ordered that his silver cup be put in Benjamin's sack. The following morning, the brothers began their journey back to Canaan.

At Joseph's command, the steward was to apprehend them and question them about the silver cup. When the steward caught up with the brothers, he seized them and searched their sacks. The steward found the cup in Benjamin's sack just as he had planted it the night before. This caused a stir amongst the brothers. However, they agreed to be escorted back to Egypt. When the Vizier (Joseph) confronted them about the silver cup, he demanded that the one who possessed the cup in his bag become his slave. In response, Judah pleaded with the Vizier that Benjamin be allowed to return to his father, and he himself be kept in Benjamin's place as a slave **(Genesis 44).**

## *Chapter VI*

# THE PROMISED LAND

### *The Holy Book within Joseph*

Judah appealed to the Vizier, begging that **Benjamin** be released and that he be enslaved in his stead because of the silver cup found in Benjamin's sack. The Vizier broke down into tears. He could not control himself any longer and so he sent the Egyptian men out of the house. Then he revealed to them that he was, in fact, their brother, Joseph. He wept so loudly that even the Egyptian household heard it outside.

The brothers were frozen and could not utter a word. He brought them closer and relayed to them the events that had happened and told them not to fear, that what they had meant for evil, God had meant for good. Then he commanded them to go and bring their father and his entire household into Egypt to live in the province of Goshen, because there were five more years of famine left.

So Joseph supplied the Egyptian transport wagons, new garments, silver money, and 20 additional donkeys carrying provisions for the journey (***Genesis 45:1-28***).

**Thus, Israel and his entire house of 70** gathered up with all their livestock and began their journey to Egypt. As they approached Egyptian territory, Judah went ahead to ask Joseph where the caravan should unload. They were directed into the province of Goshen and Joseph readied his chariot to meet his father there. It had been 22 years since Joseph had seen his father. When they met, they embraced each other and wept together for quite a while. His father then remarked, "Now let me die, since I have seen your face, because you are still alive" (**Genesis 46:1-3**4).

Afterward, Joseph's family personally met the Pharaoh of Egypt. The Pharaoh honored their stay and even proposed that if there were any qualified men in their house, then they may elect a chief herdsman to oversee Egyptian livestock. Because the Pharaoh had such a high regard for Joseph, practically making him his equal, it had been an honor to meet his father. Thus, Israel was able to bless the Pharaoh (***Genesis 47:1-47:12***).

## *Jacob's Request to Go Home to the Promised Land*

The house of Israel acquired many possessions and multiplied exceedingly during the course of 17 years, even through the worst of the seven-year famine. At this time, Joseph's father was 147 years old and bedridden. He had fallen ill and lost most of his vision. Joseph was called into his father's house and Israel pleaded with his son that he not be buried in Egypt. Rather, he requested to be carried to the land of Canaan to be buried with his forefathers. Joseph was sworn to do as his father asked of him.

**Genesis 47:27-31 (KJV)**
*²⁷And Israel dwelt in the land of Egypt, in the country of Goshen; and they had possessions therein, and grew, and multiplied exceedingly. ²⁸And Jacob lived in the land of Egypt seventeen years: so the whole age of Jacob was an hundred forty and seven years. ²⁹And the time drew nigh that Israel must die: and he called his son Joseph, and said unto him, If now I have found grace in thy sight, put, I pray thee, thy hand under my thigh, and deal kindly and truly with me;* **bury me not, I pray thee, in Egypt**: *³⁰But I will lie with my fathers, and thou shalt carry me out of Egypt, and bury me in their burying place. And he said, I will do as thou hast said. ³¹And he said, Swear unto me. And he sware unto him. And Israel bowed himself upon the bed's head.*

The biblical narrative makes a point of the renaming of the "Land of Canaan" to the "Land of Israel" as marking the Israelite conquest of the Promised Land.

The **Promised Land** is a term used to describe the land promised or given by God to the Israelites, the descendants of Jacob. The promise is firstly made to Abraham and then renewed to his son, Isaac, and to Isaac's son, Jacob (***Genesis 28:13***), Abraham's grandson. The promised land was described in terms of the territory from the River of Egypt to the Euphrates River (***Exodus 23:31***) and was given to their descendants after the Exodus (***Deuteronomy 1:8***).

**Deuteronomy 1:8 (KJV)**
*⁸Behold, I have set the land before you: go in and possess the land which the LORD sware unto your fathers, Abraham, Isaac, and Jacob, to give unto them and to their seed after them.*

## Divine Promise

The promise that is the basis of the term is contained in several verses of Genesis in the Torah. In Genesis 12:1 it is said, *"The LORD had said to Abram, "Leave your country, your people and your father's household and go to the land I will show you."*

and in Genesis 12:7: *"The LORD appeared to Abram and said, "To your offspring [or seed] I will give this land."*

Commentators note that it is to Abram's descendants that the land will (in the future tense) be given, not to Abram directly nor there and then. However, in Genesis 15:7 it is said:

*He also said to him, 'I am the LORD, who brought you out of Ur of the Chaldeans to give you this land to take possession of it.'*

And in Genesis 15:18-21, the boundary of the Promised Land is clarified in terms of the territory of various ancient peoples, as follows:

*On that day the LORD made a covenant with Abram and said, 'To your descendants I give this land, from the river of Egypt to the great river, the Euphrates—the land of the Kenites, Kenizzites, Kadmonites, Hittites, Perizzites, Rephaites, Amorites, Canaanites, Girgashites and Jebusites.'*

The verse is said to describe what are known as "borders of the land". In Jewish tradition, these borders define the maximum extent of the land promised to the descendants of Abraham through his son Isaac and grandson Jacob.

The promise was confirmed to Jacob at Genesis 28:13, though the borders are still vague and are in terms of "the land on which you are lying". Other geographical borders are given in Exodus 23:31, which describes borders as marked by the Red Sea, the "Sea of the Philistines" (i.e., the Mediterranean) and the "River" (the Euphrates).

The promise is fulfilled at the end of the Exodus from Egypt. Deuteronomy 1:8 says:

*See, I have given you this land. Go in and take possession of the land that the LORD swore he would give to your fathers—to Abraham, Isaac and Jacob—and to their descendants after them.*

It took a long time before the Israelites could subdue the Canaanite inhabitants of the land. The furthest extent of the Land of Israel was achieved during the time of the United Kingdom of Israel under David. The actual land controlled by the Israelites has fluctuated considerably over time and, at times, the land has been under the control of various empires. However, under Jewish tradition, even when it is not in Jewish occupation, the land has not lost its status as the Promised Land.

**Genesis 28:13 (KJV)**
[13]*And, behold, the LORD stood above it, and said, I am the LORD God of Abraham thy father, and the God of Isaac: the land whereon thou liest, to thee will I give it, and to thy seed;*

The Promised Land is not real estate. The Promised Land is the lost tribes. The "lost tribes" is our DNA, which belongs to "olive" God's children. This land cannot be given to anyone or taken away by anyone. There is no war that can take away this land from any soul. We are all seeds of God. God has promised us that we would someday return to the Promised Land. That day has arrived for anyone who can find it through the "Holy Book".

We each have our own land—it is the field, the quantum field where we all reside.

Later, Joseph came to visit his father having with him his two sons, Ephraim and Manasseh. Israel declared that they would be heirs to the inheritance of the house of Israel, as if they were his own children, just as Reuben and Simeon were. Then Israel laid his left hand on the eldest Mannasseh's head and his right hand on the youngest Ephraim's head and blessed Joseph. However, Joseph was displeased that his father's right hand was not on the head of his firstborn, so he switched his father's hands. But Israel refused, saying, "but truly his younger brother shall be greater than he,"—a declaration he made just as Israel himself was to his firstborn brother Esau. To Joseph, he gave a portion more of Canaanite property than he had to his other sons, land that he fought for against the Amorites (**Genesis 48:1-22**).

Then Israel called all of his sons in and prophesied their blessings or curses to all 12 of them in order of their ages. To Joseph, he declared:

*Joseph is a fruitful bough, a fruitful bough by a well; His branches run over the wall. The archers have bitterly grieved him, Shot at him and hated him. But his bow remained in strength, And the arms of his hands were made strong by the hands of the Mighty God of Jacob (From there is the Shepherd, the Stone of Israel), By the God of your father who will help you, And by the Almighty who will bless you with blessings of heaven above, Blessings of the deep that lies beneath, Blessings of the breasts and of the womb. The blessings of your father have excelled the blessings of my ancestors, Up to the utmost bound of the everlasting hills. They shall be on the head of Joseph, And on the crown of the head of him who was separate from his brothers.*

After relaying his prophecies, Israel died. The family, including the Egyptians, **mourned him 70 days.** Joseph had his father embalmed, a process that took 40 days. Then he prepared a great ceremonial journey to Canaan leading the servants of the Pharaoh, and the elders of the houses Israel and Egypt beyond the Jordan River. They stopped at Atad where they observed seven days of mourning. Here, their lamentation was so great that it caught the attention of surrounding Canaanites who remarked, "This is a deep mourning of the Egyptians." So they named this spot Abel Mizraim. Then Joseph buried Israel in the cave of Machpelah, the property of Abraham when he bought it from the Hittites (***Genesis 49:33-50:14***).

After their father died, the brothers of Joseph feared retribution for being responsible for Joseph's deliverance into Egypt as a slave. **Joseph wept as they spoke and told them that what had happened was God's purpose to save lives and the lives of his family**. He comforted them and their ties were reconciled.

**Genesis 50:15-21 (KJV)**
*[15]And when Joseph's brethren saw that their father was dead, they said, Joseph will peradventure hate us, and will certainly requite us all the evil which we did unto him. [16]And they sent a messenger unto Joseph, saying, Thy father did command before he died, saying, [17]So shall ye say unto Joseph, **Forgive**, I pray thee now, the trespass of thy brethren, and their sin; for they did unto thee evil: and now, we pray thee, forgive the trespass of the servants of the God of thy father. And Joseph wept when they spake unto him. [18]And his brethren also went and fell down before his face; and they said, Behold, we be thy servants. [19]And Joseph said unto them, **Fear not**: for am I in the place of God? [20]But as for you, ye thought evil against me; but **God meant it unto good**, to bring to pass, as it is this day, to **save much people** alive. [21]Now therefore **fear ye not**: I will nourish you and your little ones. And he comforted them, and spake kindly unto them.*

## *Joseph's Request to Go Home to the Promised Land*

Joseph lived to the age of 110, living to see his great-grandchildren. Before he died, **he made the children of Israel swear that when they left the land of Egypt they would take his bones** with them, and on his death his body was embalmed and placed in a coffin in Egypt (***Genesis 50:22-26***).

The children of Israel remembered their oath, and when they left Egypt during the Exodus, **Moses took Joseph's bones with him** (***Exodus 13:19***).

*[19]And Moses took the bones of Joseph with him: for he had straitly sworn the children of Israel, saying, God will surely visit you; and ye shall carry up my bones away hence with you.*

## *Jacob's Ladder—Sons of Jacob to Rise or Climb Out of Bondage*

*Genesis 28*
*¹²And he dreamed, and behold a ladder set up on the Earth, and the top of it reached to heaven: and behold the angels of God ascending and descending on it.*

*Genesis 28:10-22 (KJV)*
*¹⁰And Jacob went out from Beersheba, and went toward Haran. ¹¹And he lighted upon a certain place, and tarried there all night, because the sun was set; and he took of the stones of that place, and put them for his pillows, and lay down in that place to sleep. ¹²And he dreamed, and behold a ladder set up on the Earth, and the top of it reached to heaven: and behold the angels of God ascending and descending on it.*

*¹³And, behold, the LORD stood above it, and said, I am the LORD God of Abraham thy father, and the God of Isaac: the land whereon thou liest, to thee will I give it, and to thy seed; ¹⁴And thy seed shall be as the dust of the Earth, and thou shalt spread abroad to the west, and to the east, and to the north, and to the south: and in thee and in thy seed shall all the families of the Earth be blessed.*

*¹⁵And, behold, I am with thee, and will keep thee in all places whither thou goest, and will bring thee again into this land; for I will not leave thee, until I have done that which I have spoken to thee of. ¹⁶**And Jacob awaked out of his sleep, and he said, Surely the LORD is in this place; and I knew it not.** ¹⁷And he was afraid, and said, How dreadful is this place! this is none other but the house of God, and this is the gate of heaven. ¹⁸And Jacob rose up early in the morning, and took the stone that he had put for his pillows, and set it up for a pillar, and poured **oil** upon the top of it. ¹⁹And he called the name of that place Bethel: but the name of that city was called Luz at the first.*

*²⁰And Jacob vowed a vow, saying, If God will be with me, and will keep me in this way that I go, and will give me bread to eat, and raiment to put on, ²¹So that I come again to my father's house in peace; then shall the LORD be my God: ²²And this stone, which I have set for a pillar, shall be God's house: and of all that thou shalt give me I will surely give the tenth unto thee.*

## The Land of the Christ Consciousness

Christ consciousness is *"the awareness within each soul, imprinted in pattern on the mind and waiting to be awakened by the will, of the soul's oneness with God."*—**Edgar Cayce**

Arriving in the big open sea, a field of treasures unimaginable to the human eye is the "promised land" where all souls reside. Our compassion allowing and loving others enough to accept the magnitude of their experiences is the key ingredient required to enter The Kingdom of Heaven within The Holy Book of The Great Invisible Spirit.☺

Through compassion, we're able to accept all experiences without judgment. Through this great allowing, we make room for completeness in our own lives.

Understanding our thoughts, feelings, emotions—using negative experiences and emotions as our partners and as opportunities to release any basic fear-based beliefs, we can come to KNOW and LOVE our true compassionate spiritual beings.

We have today and have always had direct access to the light and information of our bodies and our outer world—The Great Invisible Spirit. We each have our own unique divine signature of light—our "soul-song".

Our thoughts, feelings, emotions and beliefs affect ***the world beyond our own bodies***. We exist throughout time and space into infinity.

## Spiritual Being VS Human Being

Spiritual Being: A spiritual being or soul is constant and never dies—the soul lives into eternity and infinity. Your spiritual being is the sum of all of your experiences since your creation with "Source—the Creator". When the soul leaves the physical form it returns to spirit form☺

Human Being: A human being or physical being is temporary—the physical body dies. It is what our spiritual being (soul) enters into upon being born into a body on Earth. The word "tent" referenced in the Bible means our physical body or our house where the soul resides.

When we are in our human bodies, we experience many thoughts and feelings as we do in our spirit form. Our thoughts and feelings are experienced throughout our entire spiritual being, including the physical body we are living in.

We as spiritual beings have lived in many other physical bodies throughout our nonlinear life. We have come to experience life here over and over again, to learn love and compassion through living and experiencing in Earth's three-dimensional life experience, which is limiting and sometimes filled with pain and sorrow.

# PART V

# *The Holy Book*

**Psalm 37:29** (KJV)
[29] The righteous shall inherit the land, and dwell therein for ever.

## Chapter 9

# EVERYTHING IS CONNECTED

### *"I Feel Therefore I AM" Sanetha*

*Feelings* are the most powerful force in the Universe. Compassion is the force that connects everything to the Universe—into infinity.

When you cry, all of you cries. When you laugh, all of you laughs. When you release negativity, all of you releases negativity. When you feel love, all of you *feels* love. When you connect, all of you connects.

Imagine now all of us feeling love all at the same time uniting as "ONE", creating "World Peace". You are connected to everything, connected to "All That Is"—The Creator.

You have life experiences—some good, some not so good. You now have an opportunity to release what no longer serves you. When you reconnect to the **"Great Invisible Spirit"** within the **"Holy Book"**, you will enter into the **"Kingdom of Heaven"** and still be living in your house or physical being here on Earth.

My soul purpose is the same today as it was yesterday and will be again tomorrow. I have reincarnated many times, carrying with me the same message. Each time I bring the message, it is better than the time before—as is all of my gifts and abilities. The message I bring is the knowledge of and ability to live in Heaven or Paradise on Earth.

If you want to change something in the world, become the change you wish to see—fill up your heart with compassion and unconditional love and then happily send it out into the Universe like a dove delivering peace and good will to all. *Feelings* are far more effective than thinking. We've been conditioned to believe that *feelings* and emotions are ineffective.

## *The Chakras*

**What is a chakra?** Chakras are energy centers in our bodies. They are the openings for "life energy" to flow in and out of our aura. Their function is to nourish and vitalize our physical body and aid awareness to the development of our consciousness. Each one contains data referring to our past, present and future thoughts, feelings and emotions. Every chakra in our body vibrates at a different speed, producing multiple colors in our aura.

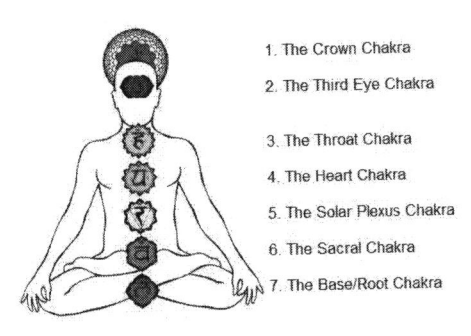

1. The Crown Chakra
2. The Third Eye Chakra
3. The Throat Chakra
4. The Heart Chakra
5. The Solar Plexus Chakra
6. The Sacral Chakra
7. The Base/Root Chakra

The concept of *chakra* originates in Hindu texts and is featured in tantric and yogic traditions of Hinduism and Buddhism. Its name derives from the Sanskrit word for "wheel" or "turning".

The chakras are believed to be a number of wheel-like vortices that, according to traditional Indian medicine, exist in the surface of the subtle body of living beings. The chakras are said to be "force centers" or whorls of energy permeating from a point in the physical body, with the layers of the subtle bodies in an ever-increasing fan-shaped formation. Rotating vortices of subtle matter, they are considered focal points for the reception and transmission of energies. Different belief systems put forward a varying number of chakras; the best-known system in the West has seven chakras, although like everything else, all energy evolves, including the chakras.

Now, in the beginning of the New Age, with new energy, new opportunities and new choices, everything is evolving and being promoted to a new state of "being". It is typical for chakras to be depicted as either flower-like or wheel-like. In the former case, "petals" are shown around the perimeter of a circle. In the later, spokes divide the circle into segments, making the chakra resemble a wheel (or "chakra"). Each chakra possesses a specific number of segments or petals.

## *DNA BLUEPRINTS and ELEMENTS*

Some people are very fixed in holding onto the old beliefs, and others are more willing to open up to the new understanding. We are connected to our source, which is the Creator God. We are all part of God; we originated as God-sparks created by "Source".

We carry our DNA with us from lifetime to lifetime. Most of the DNA is not being used and science has not yet discovered why it exists—*"there is a reason for everything".*

There are messages encoded in our DNA, including the unused portion of your DNA. The divine timing of the divine plan has arrived to live a life in paradise or in Heaven on Earth.

The 144 DNA Blueprints make up energy streams in our DNA. There are 144 DNA Blueprints correlating to the 144 elements used in the periodic table. Science has not yet discovered all 144 of the elements, nor has anyone connected our DNA to them. ☺

All the elements are there waiting to be discovered, ready for send off. All of the DNA Blueprints are also waiting and ready to be uncovered, ready for ascension.

The DNA isn't dormant—it is active, vibrating, and breathing just like you. Nobody can take this away from you and it is worth more than all of the gold in the Universe. It is yours and you can use it if you chose it. It is the "Promised Land".

Within the energy streams of your DNA Blueprint are amazing gifts and abilities waiting for you. This is an awakening you will experience and it is expected to occur for the masses of people who are raising their vibrations to match the New Earth.

Rebirth or resurrection means allowing the mind, body and spirit to shift to a higher expression of itself. Through the conscious use of choice and free will, man is greater than his fear or superficial limitations.

Choosing, aligning, and allowing a spiritual transformation to take place are the first steps required to move forward on your path and into ascension of the fifth dimension.

The ancients knew that higher frequencies enhance the possibility of ascension. As true initiates, spiritual beings having a human experience, we all have achieved a certain mastery to be here on Earth during this "Cosmic" event—a major historical event.

Earth will no longer tolerate fear, hate, condemnation or archaic beliefs. The New Earth will support only highly evolved frequencies—thus, one must release what no longer serves them in order to become a clear, clean vessel. This was the gift of the Creator—to anchor the coded information of this consciousness and all of its possibilities.

Our world is in position for the most spectacular transformations in the year of 2012 and beyond. The nature of these transformations will be beyond our ability to comprehend, but will become increasingly more apparent in due time. Our world as we have come to know it is in the midst of the most profound changes. We have grown accustomed to living a life affected around totally false impressions that many so strongly believe in.

## In My Father's House are Many Mansions

### The KINGDOM OF HEAVEN within THE HOLY BOOK of THE GREAT INVISISLBE SPIRIT

*John 14:1-31 (KJV)*
$^1$Let not your heart be troubled: ye believe in God, believe also in me. $^2$In my Father's house are many mansions: if it were not so, I would have told you. I go to prepare a place for you. $^3$And if I go and prepare a place for you, I will come again, and receive you unto myself; that where I am, there ye may be also. $^4$And whither I go ye know, and the way ye know. $^5$Thomas saith unto him, Lord, we know not whither thou goest; and how can we know the way? $^6$Jesus saith unto him, I am the way, the truth, and the life: no man cometh unto the Father, but by me. $^7$If ye had known me, ye should have known my Father also: and from henceforth ye know him, and have seen him. $^8$Philip saith unto him, Lord, show us the Father, and it sufficeth us. $^9$Jesus saith unto him, Have I been so long time with you, and yet hast thou not known me, Philip? he that hath seen me hath seen the Father; and how sayest thou then, Show us the Father? $^{10}$Believest thou not that I am in the Father, and the Father in me? the words that I speak unto you I speak not of myself: but the Father that dwelleth in me, he doeth the works. $^{11}$Believe me that I am in the Father, and the Father in me: or else believe me for the very works' sake. $^{12}$Verily, verily, I say unto you, He that believeth on me, the works that I do shall he do also; and greater works than these shall he do; because I go unto my Father. $^{13}$And whatsoever ye shall ask in my name, that will I do, that the Father may be glorified in the Son. $^{14}$If ye shall ask any thing in my name, I will do it. $^{15}$If ye love me, keep my commandments. $^{16}$And I will pray the Father, and he shall give you another Comforter, that he may abide with you for ever; $^{17}$Even the Spirit of truth; whom the world cannot receive, because it seeth him not, neither knoweth him: but ye know him; for he dwelleth with you, and shall be in you. $^{18}$I will not leave you comfortless: I will come to you. $^{19}$Yet a little while, and the world seeth me no more; but ye see me: because I live, ye shall live also. $^{20}$At that day ye shall know that I am in my Father, and ye in me, and I in you. $^{21}$He that hath my commandments, and keepeth them, he it is that loveth me: and he that loveth me shall be loved of my Father, and I will love him, and will

manifest myself to him. ²²Judas saith unto him, not Iscariot, Lord, how is it that thou wilt manifest thyself unto us, and not unto the world? ²³Jesus answered and said unto him, If a man love me, he will keep my words: and my Father will love him, and we will come unto him, and make our abode with him. ²⁴He that loveth me not keepeth not my sayings: and the word which ye hear is not mine, but the Father's which sent me. ²⁵These things have I spoken unto you, being yet present with you. ²⁶But the Comforter, which is the Holy Ghost, whom the Father will send in my name, he shall teach you all things, and bring all things to your remembrance, whatsoever I have said unto you. ²⁷Peace I leave with you, my peace I give unto you: not as the world giveth, give I unto you. Let not your heart be troubled, neither let it be afraid. ²⁸Ye have heard how I said unto you, I go away, and come again unto you. If ye loved me, ye would rejoice, because I said, I go unto the Father: for my Father is greater than I. ²⁹And now I have told you before it come to pass, that, when it is come to pass, ye might believe. ³⁰Hereafter I will not talk much with you: for the prince of this world cometh, and hath nothing in me. ³¹But that the world may know that I love the Father; and as the Father gave me commandment, even so I do. Arise, let us go hence.

## The Pineal Gland

"And Jacob called the name of the place Peniel: for I have seen God face to face."—**Genesis 32:30 (KJV**

*Genesis 32:24-31 (KJV)*
²⁴*And Jacob was left alone; and there wrestled a man with him until the breaking of the day. ²⁵And when he saw that he prevailed not against him, he touched the hollow of his thigh; and the hollow of Jacob's thigh was out of joint, as he wrestled with him.*

²⁶*And he said, Let me go, for the day breaketh. And he said, I will not let thee go, except thou bless me. ²⁷And he said unto him, What is thy name? And he said, Jacob. ²⁸And he said, Thy name shall be called no more Jacob, but Israel: for as a prince hast thou power with God and with men, and hast prevailed. ²⁹And Jacob asked him, and said, Tell*

*me, I pray thee, thy name. And he said, Wherefore is it that thou dost ask after my name? And he blessed him there.*

*³⁰**And Jacob called the name of the place Peniel: for I have seen God face to face, and my life is preserved. ³¹And as he passed over Penuel the sun rose upon him, and he halted upon his thigh.***

## The Third Eye

The **third eye** (also known as the **inner eye**) is a mystical and esoteric concept referring in part to the ajna (brow) chakra in certain dharmic spiritual traditions, in particular Hinduism. This concept was later adopted by Christian mystics and spiritualists as well as people from other religious faiths. It is also spoken of as the gate that leads within to inner realms and spaces of higher consciousness. Among Christian mystics, the term is used in a broad sense to indicate a non-dualistic perspective.

In New Age spirituality, the third eye may alternately symbolize a state of enlightenment or the evocation of mental images having deeply personal spiritual or psychological significance. The third eye is often associated with visions, clairvoyance (which includes the ability to observe chakras and auras), precognition, and out-of-body experiences. People who have allegedly developed the capacity to utilize their third eyes are sometimes known as *seers*.

# Chapter 99

# WEAVING THE PIECES

### *"I Think Therefore I Am"*

On the night of 10—11 November 1619, while stationed in Neuburg an der Donau, Germany, Descartes experienced a series of three powerful dreams or visions that he later claimed profoundly influenced his life. He concluded from these visions that the pursuit of science would prove to be, for him, the pursuit of true wisdom and a central part of his life's work. Descartes also saw very clearly that all truths were linked with one another, so that finding a fundamental truth and proceeding with logic would open the way to all science. This basic truth, Descartes found quite soon—his famous "I think" statement.

Descartes began his long correspondence with Princess Elisabeth of Bohemia (John the Baptist's mother in another life and the son of Joseph in another), which was devoted mainly to moral and psychological subjects. Connected with this correspondence, in 1649 he published *Les Passions de l'âme* (*Passions of the Soul*), that he dedicated to the Princess.

René Descartes (March 31, 1596—February 11, 1650) was a French philosopher, mathematician, scientist and writer who spent most of his adult life in the Dutch Republic. He has been dubbed the "Father of Modern Philosophy" and much of subsequent Western philosophy is a response to his writings, which continue to be studied closely to this day.

Descartes frequently set his views apart from those of his predecessors. In the opening section of the *Passions of the Soul*, a treatise on the early modern version of what are now commonly called emotions, he goes so far as to assert that he will write on his topic *"as if no one had written on these matters before".*

Descartes suggested that the pineal gland is "the seat of the soul" for several reasons. First, the soul is unitary (undivided and existing as a unit), and unlike many areas of the brain, the pineal gland appeared to be unitary (though subsequent microscopic inspection has revealed it is formed of two hemispheres). Second, Descartes observed that the pineal gland was located near the ventricles. He believed the animal spirits of the ventricles acted through the nerves to control the body and that the pineal gland influenced this process.

Descartes is often regarded as the first thinker to emphasize the use of reason to develop the natural sciences. For him, philosophy was a thinking system that embodied all knowledge and expressed it in this way:

*"Thus, all Philosophy is like a tree, of which Metaphysics is the root, Physics the trunk, and all the other sciences the branches that grow out of this trunk, which are reduced to three principal, namely, Medicine, Mechanics, and Ethics. By the science of Morals, I understand the highest and most perfect which, presupposing an entire knowledge of the other sciences, is the last degree of wisdom."*

The **pineal gland** (also called the pineal body, epiphysis cerebri, epiphysis, conarium or the "third eye") is a small endocrine gland in the vertebrate brain. It produces the serotonin derivative melatonin, a hormone that affects the modulation of wake/sleep patterns and seasonal functions. Its shape resembles a tiny pine cone (hence its name) and it is located near the centre of the brain, between the two hemispheres, tucked in a groove where the two rounded thalamic bodies join.

Rene Descartes saw very clearly that all truths were linked with one another, so that finding a fundamental truth and proceeding with logic would open the way to all science. Indeed, the deep seated truth and logic taking place is opening the way to all science. Rene has always existed—continuing his work and his message using a different set of experiences, possibilities and probabilities. He, too, has returned a better Rene than he was the day before.

The DNA/Blueprint is always with you—the spiritual being. Each time you incarnate into a physical body, you—the Great Invisible Spirit within your DNA—automatically have all of your life experiences as part of you.

We are multidimensional, infinite beings. Our soul comes and goes, always carrying our personality, our unique DNA/Blueprint. The soul seeks to reside in tents, houses, temples—human bodies ☺—to gain or increase his light and information through experiences the soul needs to learn certain lessons as an individual and as one with the other souls.

The DNA/Blueprint carries your unique signature of information and light. The information is all your lifetimes of experiences including your gifts and abilities. The light is your level of enlightenment or your light quotient that you possess.

Less than 10% of our DNA is being used for building proteins. The other 90% are considered "junk DNA." It is this junk DNA—that we can now have full use of if we so choose. Not everyone will choose to "AWAKEN" the sleeping DNA. It is active—all you need to do is turn it on—oil is required. ☺ It is a spiritual journey; no two spiritual paths are the same. You are unique and very special.

The human DNA is a biological Internet and superior in many aspects to the artificial one. The latest Russian scientific research directly or indirectly explains phenomena such as clairvoyance, intuition, spontaneous and remote acts of healing, self-healing, affirmation techniques, unusual light/auras around people (namely spiritual masters), the mind's influence on weather patterns and much more.

According to their findings, our DNA is not only responsible for the construction of our body but also serves as data storage and communication. They found that the genetic code—especially in the apparent "useless" 90%—follows the same rules as all our human languages.

Of course, the frequency has to be correct. And this is why not everybody is equally successful or can do it with always the same strength. The individual person must work on the inner processes and development—in other words, work on their spiritual development—in order to establish a conscious communication with the DNA. During a spiritual awakening, the individual will tune into the planetary/universal/galactic frequencies and increase their own vibration.

These are tunnel connections between entirely different areas in the Universe through which information can be transmitted outside of space and time. The DNA attracts these bits of information and passes them on to our consciousness. This process of hyper-communication (telepathy, channeling) is most effective in a state of relaxation.

The higher developed an individual's consciousness is, the more the individual can connect to the 90% of the DNA that is not being used, which science calls "junk DNA". Anyone can achieve these results through their spiritual awakening to The Kingdom of Heaven within the Holy Book of the Great Invisible Spirit. ☺

Stress, worry or an agitated emotion prevent successful communication or the information will be totally distorted and useless. In humans, communication is most often encountered when one suddenly gains access to information that is outside one's knowledge base. Such communication is then experienced as inspiration, intuition and physic abilities.

In earlier times, humanity had been very strongly connected to group consciousness and thereby acted as a group. These much earlier times existed during Atlantis and Lemuria. Many do not know about these civilizations before the time of Adam and Eve—before the change of our DNA.

Lemuria, which existed before Atlantis, was on the Pacific Coast and Atlantis on the East Coast. Both of these continents will rise out of the ocean in this lifetime.

There have been Golden Ages before, but none like the one we have entered into NOW! The world is not ending on December 21st, 2012. It is an END of TIMES, an end of the old times and a beginning to the NEW.

The term **Golden Age** comes from Greek mythology and legend and refers to the first in a sequence of four or five (or more) Ages of Man, in which the Golden Age is first, followed in sequence by the Silver, Bronze and Iron Ages and then the present, a period of decline. By extension, "Golden Age" denotes a period of primordial peace, harmony, stability and prosperity.

## *Sleeping DNA*

**Romans 11 (KJV)**
*[8](According as it is written, God hath given them the spirit of slumber, eyes that they should not see, and ears that they should not hear;) unto this day.*

Before the deluge, during other civilizations, we (son of man) had a higher vibration. We were much more advanced spiritually; our technology was also more advanced. There were energies on the planet that gave us the ability to be a higher evolved being. Like me, you may have been one of those spiritual beings in one or more of these lifetimes. These energies were destroyed except for some that were stored away in a safe place by highly evolved spiritual beings—until such a time as it is NOW when the Earth, the Universe and the Cosmos would come into alignment to allow the Earth and humanity to raise their vibration to ascend into the fifth dimension.

Our will—free will and choice—allows these energies to awaken *the Great Invisible Spirit* to claim your experiences, knowledge, wisdom, gifts and abilities collected from all of your lifetimes.

## Oil—Our Will

The energy is NOW available. You have within you a huge amount of DNA that has been waiting for this spectacular "galactic" time! Accessing the energy and turning it on, so to speak, involves your spiritual awakening. Through the Universal Law of Free Will and Choice, you can choose to claim what is yours. All you have to do is acknowledge within that you want to claim your God-given divinity and begin your personal journey to freedom.

### Malachi 4 KJV
*¹For, behold, the day cometh, that shall burn as an oven; and all the proud, yea, and all that do wickedly, shall be stubble: and the day that cometh shall burn them up, saith the LORD of hosts, that it shall leave them neither root nor branch. ²But unto you that fear my name shall the Sun of righteousness arise with healing in his wings; and ye shall go forth, and grow up as calves of the stall. ³And ye shall tread down the wicked; for they shall be ashes under the soles of your feet in the day that I shall do this, saith the LORD of hosts. ⁴Remember ye the law of Moses my servant, which I commanded unto him in Horeb for all Israel, with the statutes and judgments. ⁵Behold, I will send you Elijah the prophet before the coming of the great and dreadful day of the LORD: ⁶And he shall turn the heart of the fathers to the children, and the heart of the children to their fathers, lest I come and smite the earth with a curse.*

It is true that our physical bodies use less than 10% of our **DNA**. The rest of our **DNA** has been termed "junk DNA". Understand that the junk DNA is simply the option for improvement or upgrade—by individuals using their "oil", upgrades will occur if the house has been cleaned.

First of all, with the help of Wikipedia, let me define **DNA** in simple terms—it's not like I am a French scientist or something, at least not in this lifetime. ☺

**DNA**, short for **deoxyribonucleic acid**, is the molecule that contains the genetic **code** of organisms. This includes animals, plants, protists, archaea and bacteria.

**DNA** is in each cell in the organism and tells cells what proteins to make. A cell's proteins determine its function. **DNA is inherited by children from their parents**. This is why children share traits with their parents, such as skin, hair and eye color. The DNA in a person is a combination of the DNA from each of their parents.

This is the small portion of the DNA that science refers to as active DNA—the DNA that we currently use. The active DNA—the basic code that is inherited by children from their parents—the dormant DNA, the larger portion of the DNA, is not inherited by children from their parents because we usually have different parents for each incarnation. ☺

The unused **DNA** is part of your **BLUEPRINT** brought into your physical body when you incarnated. The unused or dormant DNA is "light and information"—your light quotient that carries all of your gifts, abilities and experiences from all of your lifetimes.

Your DNA (your seed), such as grain or manna, remains dormant until it is given a stimulus to grow such as soil, water and sunlight— and, of course, oil and, most importantly, unconditional love.

Draw a circle and put a dot (seed) in the middle of it. This diagram represents your **BLUEPRINT.**

The dot is the part of the DNA Blueprint that is being used (less than 10%). This dot is the basic code that carries the basic tools you chose for this lifetime. These tools were carefully selected by you and other soul family members before you incarnated into this life. The tools direct what kind of life experiences you will have to accomplish or learn in order to complete your purpose. Many of these soul family members who helped you choose also chose to reincarnate into this life and may be closely related or maybe you haven't met them yet.

You knew before incarnating that you would be separated from the majority of your identity and that you wouldn't remember who you were or where you came from. Part of your basic toolkit holds those two questions.

We are time sensitive in a way that when it is our time to awaken, the bells and whistles start to blow. Not all hear or see what is going on. The soul family members who did not reincarnate at this time—who are in soul state on the other side of the veil—can *see* you, *hear* you and, yes, *feel* you, too! Some of us can see, hear and feel them. More and more of us are starting to wake up.

The seed or the dot will expand as you grow while learning lessons in this life. However, the other DNA, the over 90% that is not being used, is sealed for the time being. As you grow spiritually, the seed is nourished.

As **The Great Invisible Spirit** awakens, you will access more and more of your gifts, abilities, knowledge and wisdom that is lying dormant within your being. The circle is your soul's journey—life times of experiences past, present and future. YOU are a unique, energetic signature within the blueprint. No two souls have the exact same signature.

When you leave this physical body, the seed/spiritual being becomes a fully awakened **GREAT INVISIBLE SPIRIT**☺ and returns to "SOURCE" or "ALL THAT IS".

It has been a very long time coming—**the "New Energy", Fifth-Dimensional Energy** is here online in alignment and available to those who choose to raise their vibrations to match the new energy on the planet.

You are **The Great Invisible Spirit** who by "our will" (oil) can advance to the Kingdom of Heaven within The Holy Book.

## *Your Divine Blueprint*

Your divine blueprint travels with you from lifetime to lifetime. It cannot be destroyed and nothing can take that away from you. It is infinite. You are an infinite being existing in many dimensions.

While I was cruising in the Bahamas this year, a place where I had never been before in this lifetime, yet a place that is part of my "Akashic Record" and my DNA blueprint, I brought Kryon—Book 12 along with me called ***The Twelve Layers of DNA (An Esoteric Study of the Mastery Within.*** I wanted to share this beautiful quote from page 253, part of a channeling message from Kryon channeled through the author Lee Carroll, who has given permission to print up to 500 words of his book.

> "Can you feel the love of God here? If you can, it's a good beginning. I'll tell you this; if you can *feel* this message, you can accomplish what it teaches. This healing doesn't happen all at once, but I'll give you the method. Each one of you is unique on the planet. Each one has a life lesson that is unique. Each one has a unique pattern of lives lived in the past. That means your Akashic Record is like no one else's and your Higher-Self is also unique. This limits my ability to give you some kind of 3D generic list or way to heal yourself, since you are dealing with the specifics of "you". So instead, why not sit down in a quiet moment, with purity, and say to Spirit,

> *I would like these things. I give permission to activate the energies that needed to be activated in my life, to accomplish the purposes I came for. I want to have joy in my life, and to find the joy in my full Akash, for I deserve it and I've earned it. I've had positive, joyful lives, so I want to pull on that energy. I want to inform my DNA that I am a master!"*

Thank you Kryon . . . and thank you Lee. I am grateful for all you have done for me—Love & Light, Sanetha

## Missing Link Not Missing

We are what we have been waiting for. Our soul journey is a continuous, nonlinear experience of all our lifetimes. Our soul carries our unique signature—our **DNA** pattern or **BLUEPRINT** from lifetime to lifetime. The word **DNA** is too limiting to describe the magnificence of all of this. ☺

There are a total of **144 BLUEPRINTS**. Each blueprint is different and is comprised of the infinite source field. We each are part of one of the 144 blueprints.

Within each **BLUEPRINT** there are thousands of **SOUL GROUP ENERGIES**. Each soul has a purpose of trying to ascend into our SOUL GROUP ENERGY. Within each of the **SOUL GROUP ENERGIES** are all of ISRAEL's children, the lambs, "flocks of sheep" or spiritual beings who have not yet ascended to one of the Blueprint groups.

As a soul, our goal is to access 100% of the Soul Group Energy. Then the next goal is to access 100% of the Blueprint. Most of our Blueprint is dormant, but it is activated. It needs to be awakened. ☺

The Glands are the doorways into the Blueprint, yet encompass everything—the DNA solidification of the Blueprint—the Holy Grail right under your nose☺. The secret or activity of the pineal gland is only relatively understood. Historically, its location deep in the brain suggested to philosophers that it possessed particular importance. This combination led to its being a "mystery" gland with myth, superstition and occult theories surrounding its perceived functions.

Rene Descartes, who dedicated much time to the study of the pineal gland, called it the "principal seat of the soul." According to Wikipedia, he believed that it was the point of connection between the intellect and the body. Descartes attached significance to the gland because he believed it to be the only section of the brain that existed as a single part, rather than one half of a pair. He argued that because (he thought) a person can never have "more than one thought at a time", external stimuli must be united within the brain before being considered by the soul, and he considered the pineal gland to be situated in "the most suitable possible place for this purpose", located centrally in the brain and surrounded by branches of the carotid arteries.

*"My view is that this gland is the principal seat of the soul, and the place in which all our thoughts are formed."*—**Rene Descartes**

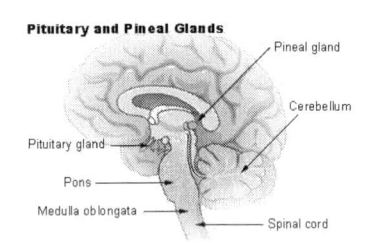

**Pituitary and Pineal Glands**

- Pineal gland
- Cerebellum
- Pituitary gland
- Pons
- Medulla oblongata
- Spinal cord

When a soul has lived as a scientist in one life and a spiritualist in another life, the knowledge and abilities accumulated over your soul's journey that have been separated from you at birth can now be reunited without your soul vacating the physical body.

This is the Golden Age—once you ignite your light, the process will begin. Come along if you choose to, for we have much work to do—lifetimes of clearing the hay, sheering off and burning away what no longer serves you. Adam and Eve come out where ever you are, hang up those old leaves because you don't need them anymore. It is time to dump all the fear, the worry, the jealousy, the hatred—all that stuff will simply be gone if you are willing to do the work.

I always knew that I was here to do something really big and so are you! I spent years searching for what that might be. The day I made the awesome discovery led me down a path of so many more discoveries. In fact, it wasn't like I was on a path; it was more like I was at a fork in the road.

# PART VI

# The Beginning

This is the beginning of a new age, a new Earth, a new human in the new energy living in paradise or heaven on Earth. You are given an opportunity to reincarnate (reinvent) without leaving your body.

*Chapter 9*

# AN OPEN BOOK ENCODED IN THE REALMS OF LIGHT

*"My personal lifetimes of events and experiences are an open book encoded in the realms of light."*—**Sanetha**

### The Energy of Love

In this life, I have been carried home, tickled, and healed by ANGELS; I have been contacted by phone, in my dreams and in my visions by ANGELS; I have been called an ANGEL; I have seen the ANGELS come to take my father to his place in the sky; and now I KNOW our son Michael walks with ANGELS as an angelic guide.☺

Everyone you have ever known in any of your lifetimes are a breath away, waiting patiently until the day comes that you know they are standing right there. They are devoted, loving, caring and willing to help you find your way. Before you incarnated, you knew that there were universal laws that were created to ensure that all souls must have their own free will and choice.

Free will and choice allow you to decide what you want and what you don't want. This law also ensures that no other soul can do another soul's lessons. This includes the spirit souls on the other side who are standing right beside you. They cannot interfere with your free will and choice. That is why they cannot help you until you ask them. ☺

They have never left—like you, they are multidimensional and expand throughout the Universes. Since thoughts are energy, they hear your thoughts. This is something that you too can do if you so wish—just use oil and manna. ☺

Tune into the frequency of **"LOVE"** and begin a new creation of your reality. Your point of power is in the present where the new energy of your thoughts and feelings exist in a better, stronger and much clearer way than they existed in the previous old, very dense energy.

I have come to communicate my thoughts, which carry a much higher frequency than the thoughts I have communicated in previous lifetimes. I have tuned into an energy that can only manifest using oil. ☺

This energy is called love—unconditional love. It has been the most sought-after energy on the planet—the Holy Grail, the Holy Book. Everyone has it, but not everyone can find it because they cannot see it, hear it, or feel it yet.

These thoughts are not new, they are stronger—just like you. We are stronger and better than we were yesterday—and tomorrow we will be stronger and better than the time before.

There is so much more than meets the third eye!

### *Invisible to Visible: Beyond The Veil*

Vanessa, an Author, International Energy Master, Bodyworker, Teacher, and Clairvoyant Energy Reader & Intuitive Consultant, . . . a princess and my dear friend in one lifetime and a loving son in another—and she was the mother of my husband in another time in history!

She was a princess who was a master of metaphysics, analytic geometry and moral philosophy, and she had a keen interest in natural philosophy. I was a famous French mathematician, scientist and philosopher.

The Universe orchestrated our entire meeting—there is a reason for everything. Why? What are the chances of all of the details that had to play out for our meeting to take place?☺ Whenever there is a question, there is always an answer.

Our communication with "The Spirit Realm" led us to come together in this lifetime for many reasons. We are soul family—we have never been apart. We have both incarnated into this time in history to deliver messages carrying the new energy for anyone who seeks the information from the light.

We with our soul families on the other side of the veil knew that many will have many questions during their awakening to their divine identity. We wanted to provide some additional divine guidance in this book for those who are searching for answers to their questions and for those who are searching for the questions that will help steer the way on their spiritual path.

> *"Without a question—there are no answers; without an answer— there are no questions."*—***Sanetha***

**Vanessa ENERGY MASTER and INTUITIVE CONSULTANT and Sanetha SPIRITUAL HEALER and INTERPRETER—a follow up book of questions and answers from beyond. Sanetha's expertise lies in the formulation of thought-provoking and unique questions and Vanessa's expertise is the ushering in of a new awareness beyond what we thought was possible. The two come together to fuse a book with questions that you may never ask and answers that you may never find. In a past life it was Vanessa who asked the questions, and Sanetha provided the answers. But there was one question Sanetha was very disappointed for not having provided a satisfactory answer to Vanessa in that life—that is until now!**

**Be one of the first to read some of the new information never ever printed before.**

**Find more about Vanessa on her website** stairwaytohealing.com

## *Reincarnation*

**Reincarnation,** according to Wikipedia, describes the concept where the soul or spirit, after the death of the body, is believed to return to live in a new human body, or in some traditions, either as a human being, animal or plant.

*Ecclesiastes 3:2 (KJV)*
*²A time to be born, and a time to die; a time to plant, and a time to pluck up that which is planted;*

When you begin to understand "reincarnation", you will begin to understand the written word past and present. All energy moves, transforms, and evolves.

*Ecclesiastes 12:7 (KJV)*
*Then shall the dust return to the Earth as it was: and the spirit shall return unto God who gave it.*

When the truth is understood, you will easily understand that Jesus was Elijah reincarnated.☺ Elijah was the first messiah; Jesus was the second messiah.

*Hebrews 13:8 (KJV)*
*Jesus Christ is the same yesterday, today, and forever.*

The "spirit and power" of Elijah the prophet in I Kings 18 came from Yahweh, the God of Israel who consumed the offering. The "spirit and power" of John the Baptist came from Elijah. Elijah is Yahweh God! Yahweh God is Elijah.

There was an "Elijah" who has walked this Earth besides Elijah the Tishbite, and he was **not** John the Baptist!

*Matthew 11:14 (KJV)*
*¹⁴And if ye will receive it, this is Elias, which was for to come.*

## New Beginnings

The world to come is a spiritual transformation in relation to death, judgment, heaven and hell, reflecting the truth that the existing world energy is descending and will be replaced by a better world or a paradise.

**Isaiah 66:22 (KJV)**
*[22]For as the new heavens and the new earth, which I will make, shall remain before me, saith the LORD, so shall your seed and your name remain.*

What comes is not the end, but the beginning. This has always been this way—there are no endings, but always beautiful, glorious, new beginnings. Old energy disintegrates as the new energy is created (reincarnated energy). This is not the first time I have come with this message. The other messages are past life—old energy.

All beginnings come back better than the time before. Mother Gaia is in transition—before she goes and upon her reincarnation, she is calling all of her children to be by her side to receive their blessings.

The transition is not an easy one as we and our mother Earth shed our skin and morph into the beautiful butterfly. Each soul will use his own "oil and manna", while the old parts of you won't give up without a fight. The journey may become difficult, but the rewards are unlike anything you can imagine.

The dream humanity has lived for centuries ends and we awaken to a bright new day—a bright new way.

Our individual worth **comes from within**, through our spiritual development, our evolution and our divine signature—our divine DNA blueprint. Letting go and dissolving our differences, we can unite once again as one. We integrate and unify with the energy of the Universe, with the great cosmic spirit—"The Great Invisible Spirit".

Love based on anything other than the pureness of your own God-self and God the Creator changes the world, the Universe and the Galaxy as we know it. We can prepare ourselves for unity with the universal spirit.

In the Age of Aquarius, we break from the past to create the future we desire in our world and in our life. The soul transition is a reversal—a life review, downsizing and getting rid of baggage so that you might fit through your new doors.

The answers we find will be different—not because the answers have changed, but that the energy has changed, allowing you to receive the information with a new set of eyes and a new set of ears. These changes require a thorough examination of what has been and what we wish to become—who you are and where we all come from.☺

Once enlightened, each human being will continue his or her individual journey within and become reunited with the spirit self—the conscious spiritual human beings, seekers of truth. The Kingdom of Heaven within The Holy Book of the Great Invisible Spirit will bring healing to many people of many tongues and nations in the process.

## Chapter 99

# IT IS YOU WE HAVE BEEN WAITING FOR

### *The Golden Age*

The Golden Age is a period of peace, harmony, stability and prosperity.

Jesus knew of his impending death and told his disciples of the comforter who would come after him. He told them to expect the coming of the Holy Spirit, which would abide with us forever, who "... shall teach you all things, and bring all things to your remembrance, whatsoever I have said unto you" **John 14:26 (KJV)**

It is you who we've been waiting for—you are the coming of the Christ Consciousness, you are the Great Invisible Spirit who will be with us forever and ever . . .

The recognition of the Great Invisible Spirit is a necessary step on "Jacob's Ladder" throughout your journey to find the Kingdom of Heaven—the Kingdom that is spread out upon the Earth but cannot be seen by the eyes of the world. As stated in the Gospel of Thomas, "Jesus said: It (the Kingdom) will not come by expectation; they will not say, 'see here' or 'see there'. But the Kingdom of the Father is spread upon the Earth and men do not see it."

## Ascension Into the Heavens

The Gospel of John quotes Jesus as saying:

> *"No one has ascended into heaven except the one who descended from heaven, the Son of Man."*

**Confucius (551-479 BC), Chinese Philosopher**
*"When the heart is set right, then the personal life is cultivated. When the personal life is cultivated, then the home life is regulated. When the home life is regulated, the national life orderly, then the world is at peace."*

**King Solomon (circa 10$^{th}$ century BC), Biblical King of Israel**
*"Your own soul is nourished when you are kind; it is destroyed when you are cruel."*

**Proverbs 11:17 (KJV)**
*$^{17}$The merciful man doeth good to his own soul: but he that is cruel troubleth his own flesh.*

**Matthew 24 (KJV)**
*$^{1}$And Jesus went out, and departed from the temple: and his disciples came to him for to shew him the buildings of the temple. $^{2}$And Jesus said unto them, See ye not all these things? verily I say unto you, There shall not be left here one stone upon another, that shall not be thrown down. $^{3}$And as he sat upon the mount of Olives, the disciples came unto him privately, saying, Tell us, when shall these things be**? and what shall be the sign of thy coming, and of the end of the world?***

*$^{4}$And Jesus answered and said unto them, Take heed that no man deceive you. $^{5}$For many shall come in my name, saying, I am Christ; and shall deceive many. $^{6}$And ye shall hear of wars and rumours of wars: see that ye be not troubled: for all these things must come to pass, but the end is not yet. $^{7}$For nation shall rise against nation, and kingdom against kingdom: and there shall be famines, and pestilences, and earthquakes, in divers places.*

*⁸All these are the beginning of sorrows. ⁹Then shall they deliver you up to be afflicted, and shall kill you: and ye shall be hated of all nations for my name's sake. ¹⁰And then shall many be offended, and shall betray one another, and shall hate one another. ¹¹And many false prophets shall rise, and shall deceive many.*

*¹²And because iniquity shall abound, the love of many shall wax cold. ¹³But he that shall endure unto the end, the same shall be saved. ¹⁴And this gospel of the kingdom shall be preached in all the world for a witness unto all nations; and then shall the end come. ¹⁵When ye therefore shall see the abomination of desolation, spoken of by Daniel the prophet, stand in the holy place, (whoso readeth, let him understand:)*

*¹⁶Then let them which be in Judaea flee into the mountains: ¹⁷Let him which is on the housetop not come down to take any thing out of his house: ¹⁸Neither let him which is in the field return back to take his clothes. ¹⁹And woe unto them that are with child, and to them that give suck in those days!*

*²⁰But pray ye that your flight be not in the winter, neither on the sabbath day: ²¹For then shall be great tribulation, such as was not since the beginning of the world to this time, no, nor ever shall be. ²²And except those days should be shortened, there should no flesh be saved: but for the elect's sake those days shall be shortened.*

*²³Then if any man shall say unto you, Lo, here is Christ, or there; believe it not. ²⁴For there shall arise false Christs, and false prophets, and shall shew great signs and wonders; insomuch that, if it were possible, they shall deceive the very elect. ²⁵Behold, I have told you before. ²⁶Wherefore if they shall say unto you, Behold, he is in the desert; go not forth: behold, he is in the secret chambers; believe it not.*

*²⁷For as the lightning cometh out of the east, and shineth even unto the west; so shall also the coming of the Son of man be. ²⁸For wheresoever the carcase is, there will the eagles be gathered together.*

*²⁹Immediately after the tribulation of those days shall the sun be darkened, and the moon shall not give her light, and the stars shall fall from heaven, and the powers of the heavens shall be shaken:* [30]*And then shall appear the sign of the Son of man in heaven: and then shall all the tribes of the earth mourn, and they shall see the Son of man coming in the clouds of heaven with power and great glory.*

[31]*And he shall send his angels with a great sound of a trumpet, and they shall gather together his elect from the four winds, from one end of heaven to the other.* [32]*Now learn a parable of the fig tree; When his branch is yet tender, and putteth forth leaves, ye know that summer is nigh:*

[33]*So likewise ye, when ye shall see all these things, know that it is near, even at the doors.* [34]*Verily I say unto you, This generation shall not pass, till all these things be fulfilled.* [35]*Heaven and earth shall pass away, but my words shall not pass away.* [36]*But of that day and hour knoweth no man, no, not the angels of heaven, but my Father only.*

[37]*But as the days of Noah were, so shall also the coming of the Son of man be.* [38]*For as in the days that were before the flood they were eating and drinking, marrying and giving in marriage, until the day that Noe entered into the ark,* [39]*And knew not until the flood came, and took them all away; so shall also the coming of the Son of man be.*

[40]*Then shall two be in the field; the one shall be taken, and the other left.* [41]*Two women shall be grinding at the mill; the one shall be taken, and the other left.* [42]*Watch therefore: for ye know not what hour your Lord doth come.*

[43]*But know this, that if the goodman of the house had known in what watch the thief would come, he would have watched, and would not have suffered his house to be broken up.* [44]*Therefore be ye also ready: for in such an hour as ye think not the Son of man cometh.*

[45]*Who then is a faithful and wise servant, whom his lord hath made ruler over his household, to give them meat in due season?* [46]*Blessed is that servant, whom his lord when he cometh shall find so doing.* [47]*Verily I say unto you, That he shall make him ruler over all his goods.*

⁴⁸*But and if that evil servant shall say in his heart, My lord delayeth his coming;* ⁴⁹*And shall begin to smite his fellow servants, and to eat and drink with the drunken;* ⁵⁰*The lord of that servant shall come in a day when he looketh not for him, and in an hour that he is not aware of,* ⁵¹*And shall cut him asunder, and appoint him his portion with the hypocrites: there shall be weeping and gnashing of teeth.*

## The Fig Tree

**Like the leaves of the fig tree, the signs spoken** indicate the coming of "The Kingdom of Heaven within the Holy Book of The Great Invisible Spirit". The "End of Times" for Adam and Eve began when they ate the forbidden fruit and hid themselves, making clothing with the fig tree leaves because they were *seeing* for the first time through a different set of eyes.

The New Earth and the Son of Man have come around completing a full cycle, getting rid of junk in the closet and aligning with their new found energies to live a loving, joyous, prosperous life. It is now time to discard the makeshift clothing—time to come out from behind the veil into the light. No more hiding behind the fig tree leaf—it is time to *see*, *hear* and *feel* again "The Great Invisible Spirit" you really are!

**Genesis 3:7 (KJV)**
⁷*And the eyes of them both were opened, and they knew that they were naked; and they sewed fig leaves together, and made themselves aprons.*

**1 Kings 4:25 (KJV)**
²⁵*And Judah and Israel dwelt safely, every man under his vine and under his fig tree, from Dan even to Beersheba, all the days of Solomon.*

**Matthew 21:18-22 (KJV)**
¹⁸*Now in the morning as he returned into the city, he hungered.* ¹⁹*And when he saw a fig tree in the way, he came to it, and found nothing thereon, but leaves only, and said unto it, Let no fruit grow on thee henceforward for ever. And presently the fig tree withered away.* ²⁰*And*

when the disciples saw it, they marvelled, saying, How soon is the fig tree withered away! ²¹Jesus answered and said unto them, Verily I say unto you, If ye have faith, and doubt not, ye shall not only do this which is done to the fig tree, but also if ye shall say unto this mountain, Be thou removed, and be thou cast into the sea; it shall be done. ²²And all things, whatsoever ye shall ask in prayer, believing, ye shall receive.

**Matthew 3:10-12 (KJV)**

¹⁰And now also the axe is laid unto the root of the trees: therefore every tree which bringeth not forth good fruit is hewn down, and cast into the fire. ¹¹I indeed baptize you with water unto repentance. but he that cometh after me is mightier than I, whose shoes I am not worthy to bear: he shall baptize you with the Holy Ghost, and with fire: ¹²Whose fan is in his hand, and he will throughly purge his floor, and gather his wheat into the garner; but he will burn up the chaff with unquenchable fire.

## *A Reason for Everything*

The center of the brain is connected to the pineal gland, which is also known as the third eye. When you close your eyes, your third eye appears to be somewhat open; in actuality, the third eye is always open. Some souls are aware of this eye and may have a more developed insight than others. They use their third eye to see things that others not using the third eye cannot see.

Awareness and practice will develop over time using your third eye—the eye that has always been there waiting to be used just like the unused "junk" DNA. Why, then, do you suppose we lose the knowledge and the ability to use our God-given abilities? There is a reason for everything.

When you are born, the pineal gland is much larger and the size decreases during the first two years of your life. *"If you don't use it, then you lose it."* ☺

If there is coordination between the brain and the sympathetic nervous system, the intuition begins to come out of the sleep and starts to awaken—then the individual will *see* the truth with a different set of eyes.

Beautiful and harmonious images and thoughts support this kind of coordination. We must not allow negative thoughts and emotions to get in the way. These must be released and replaced with positive thoughts and emotions for the full development of the spiritual body and its organs. Being worried or anxious will hold back or block your spiritual development and reconnection to your field of dreams.

Take ownership of who you are and walk through the door to the next level, picking up the mystery pieces along your path—and at the same time be aware of and in tune to the sorrows and sufferings of others. Consciousness can be turned in many directions, but you are in the habit of directing it along one certain path, and you have forgotten your divine path.

If you consider the conscious mind that you usually use as one door, then you stand at the threshold of this mind and look out into physical reality.

By studying and exploring your own awareness, by changing the focus of your attention and using your own consciousness in as many ways as possible, you will learn what consciousness is.

When you seek within, the very effort involved extends the limitations of your consciousness, expands it, and allows the self-centered self to use its abilities, which often do not realize the God-given possessions within.

The inner senses reveal to us our own independence from physical matter, and let us recognize our unique, individual, multidimensional identity. We can live a wiser, more productive, happier physical life because we understand who we are and why we are here, individually and collectively.

In this sort of exploration, the personality attempts to go within, to find its way through the veils of adopted characteristics of its own inner identity.

The inner core of the self has telepathic and clairvoyant abilities that greatly affect family relationships and our planet. At the moment, most are not using these abilities effectively due to a loss of consciousness. These are precisely the abilities that are needed now as we enter the Golden Age. YOU create your own reality.

## Chapter 111

# UNSOLVED MYSTERIES OF THE UNIVERSE

*Thought Is Energy*

Just when I thought the book was completed, I asked if there was anything I needed to add that would benefit those reading this book? Immediately, my thoughts started to flow with the energy within. A few years ago, I bought an amazing book right after my reconnecting to my healing abilities. It is with gratitude and much love that I introduce you to this incredible gift of abundant light and information.

**The Book of Knowledge: The Keys of Enoch**—A Teaching Given on Seven Levels to be Read and Visualized in Preparation for the Brotherhood of Light to be Delivered for the Quickening of the "People of Light".

Hurtak. J. J. (1977). *The Book of Knowledge: The Keys of Enoch*. Los Gatos, CA: The Academy for Future Science. www.keysofenoch.org

It is true that when you hold the energy of this book and open it up to a random page, the information presented in front of you is the exact information you need at that time. Be amazed. The following divine information that they wanted for you, the reader of this book, is quoted from Key 3-0-1, paragraph 1.

**Key 3-0-1**
THE KEY TO FUTURE LUMINARIES AND THE KEY TO THE "DIVINE LIGHT" IS THE VEHICLE OF TIME TRANSLATION. THE "VEHICLE OF VEHICLES" IS "MERKABAH" WHICH CREATES, CONTROLS, AND HAS THE ABILITY "TO SPEAK" THROUGH ELECTROMAGNETIC SINKS. MERKABAH RE-VOLVES AND GOES, AND RISES UNDER THE HEAVEN, OR BRIGHTNESS OF THE NEXT UNIVERSE, AND ITS COURSE GOES OVER THE EARTH WITH THE "LIGHT OF ITS RAYS" INCESSANTLY INTO MYRIADS OF UNIVERSES WITHIN THE EVER UNFOLDING ETERNITY.

**Paragraph 1** *The souls who have reached the greatest levels of awareness and attunement with the Father are able to extend themselves through many dimensions of light in service to the many realms of specie intelligence desiring to know the meaning and direction of Life.*

### Heaven on Earth

The time has come for *"olive"* God's children to awaken and discover the mysteries of the Universe. Who am I? Where did I come from? Why am I here? And how do I get home again?

There are many enlightened souls who have come here to plant the seeds of change for the masses of human beings who are and will be awakened by the Great Invisible Spirit. These seeds have been carefully selected and nourished to enrich Mother Earth and all of God's children with the love, light and information so very much needed for growth and expansion at this exact time in history.

Each time we incarnate, our light and our energy is brighter and bigger than the time before. This message incarnated with the same soul who brought the message before and, like the messenger, the message is also bigger and brighter. Each time we incarnate, we come back with a new plan to accomplish our purpose—a purpose that "olive" us have been part of, that when we arrive at this place on our path, we would remember and help others who have awakened to discover their birthrights that have been sealed until the end of times. Each of us has chosen our own time to reconnect within to live in a paradise or heaven on Earth.

A *knowledge* not lost but hidden for a very long time is only available to mankind when all of the circumstances are right. When man finds the *Holy Book within "The Great Invisible Spirit"*, he will finally be home again in his Kingdom of Heaven on Earth.

**Matthew 6:10 (KJV)**
*¹⁰"Thy kingdom come, Thy will be done in earth, as it is in heaven"*

The divine soul of Elijah is a spirit who has played on this grand stage so many times throughout history, including his incarnation as Jesus. While others of light and information knew of his mission and his service to "olive" us, many more did not recognize him. There is a reason for everything.

He has come many times guided by other souls with a great purpose to awaken the masses to a new way of understanding of compassion and living—each time greater than the time before. Elijah has returned once again and this time is "clearing the hay".☺

> "God" is in "olive" us. You are a God-spark—God is part of you and you are part of God the Creator. You don't need to be anything more than you already are and you don't need money or possessions, for all your riches and treasures are within you.

> "Again, the kingdom of heaven is like unto treasure hid in a field; the which when a man hath found, he hideth, and for joy thereof goeth and selleth all that he hath, and buyeth that field."
> **—Matthew 13:44**

It is my purpose at this time, as it has been many times before, to deliver a message that has been on the minds of everyone—the beginning of the end or is it the end of the beginning? It's hard to say because just like a circle, time and space have no end and no beginning. A time of opening and understanding, a new way within this spiritual transformation is grander than you can imagine.

**Revelation 1:8 (KJV)**
*I am Alpha and Omega, the beginning and the ending, saith the Lord, which is, and which was, and which is to come, the Almighty.*

The Kingdom of Heaven is in you. You are the Great Invisible Spirit. We each have our own Holy Book to discover. Remove the "fig tree leaf" and uncover the Holy Book waiting for each of you. Are you ready to open up to the passages leading to your own spiritual truth? We each have unique gifts and abilities within our "junk" DNA—DNA that carries your personality from all of your lifetimes, just waiting to be used on this side of the veil whenever you are ready.

**The Book of Knowledge: The Keys of Enoch, Chapter 46:1-2 [1]**

There I beheld the Ancient of days whose head was like white wool, and with him another, whose countenance resembled that of a man. His countenance was full of grace, like that of one of the holy angels. Then I inquired of one of the angels, who went with me, and who showed me every secret thing, concerning this Son of man; who he was; whence he was; and why he accompanied the Ancient of days. [2] He answered and said to me, This is the Son of man, to whom righteousness belongs; with whom righteousness has dwelt; and who will reveal all the treasures of that which is concealed: for the Lord of spirits has chosen him; and his portion has surpassed all before the Lord of spirits in everlasting uprightness."

This lifetime is a continuum of all of your lifetimes that have brought you to this momentous time here on planet Earth☺ to *"reveal all the treasures of that which is concealed to whom righteousness belongs; with whom righteousness has dwelt"* The Book of Enoch 46:2.

The lesson's good and bad, we all agreed. This awakening is a birthing process, a beautiful, spiritual, blissful journey to becoming a NEW HUMAN on the NEW EARTH!

You are a spiritual being having a human experience—your body is the house for your soul to dwell. It is time to clear old energy, old templates, and let go of old belief systems—a clearing of the hay.

**John 3:5 (KJV)**
*⁵Jesus answered, Verily, verily, I say unto thee, except a man be born of water and of the Spirit, he cannot enter into the kingdom of God.*

Humanity and the Earth continue to evolve—The New Earth and her energy has arrived. These energies are a higher vibration than what we are accustomed. These energies no longer serve negative thoughts and emotions such as hatred, greed, fear, worry or judgment. If your vibration is not balanced with that of the new energy, it will become very difficult to manage and life will continue and become more and more difficult. The more you let go, the easier it will become.

***Daniel 12:4***
*". . . even to the time of the end: many shall run to and fro, and knowledge shall be increased."*

Humanity is truly entering the age of divine revelations and the mind's true liberation, which is broadly known as spiritualism. The more enlightened souls will welcome the "New Age" with its emphasis on assisting others with love, healing, compassion, kindness, truth, spirituality and enlightenment.

What comes is not the end, but the beginning. The dream humanity has lived for Centuries ends and we awaken to a bright new day, a bright new way. We integrate and unify with a higher frequency of the Universe (The Kingdom of Heaven) within "the Holy Book of the Great Invisible Spirit". ☺

***Luke 24 (KJV)***
*³⁴Saying, The Lord is risen indeed, and hath appeared to Simon. ³⁵And they told what things were done in the way, and how he was known of them in breaking of bread. ³⁶And as they thus spake, Jesus himself stood in the midst of them, and saith unto them, Peace be unto you. ³⁷But they were terrified and affrighted, and supposed that they had seen a spirit. ³⁸And he said unto them, Why are ye troubled? and why do thoughts arise in your hearts? ³⁹Behold my hands and my feet, that it is I myself: handle me, and see; for a spirit hath not flesh and bones, as ye see me have.*

## THE BEGINNING OF THE END IS NOW

In *Micah 3:11-12*, the prophet Micah said that Jerusalem would be destroyed and that "Zion"—a central part of Jerusalem—would be "plowed like a field."

Micah's prophecy is believed to have been delivered in about 730 BC (about 2700 years ago). Micah's prophecy repeats again as we begin this new cycle. As cycles repeat, so do the messages—the same message only better and bigger because it has more light, more love and more information, which allows us to see, hear and feel clearer.

**Micah 3:12 (KJV)**
*¹²Therefore shall Zion for your sake be plowed as a field, and Jerusalem shall become heaps, and the mountain of the house as the high places of the forest.*

Therefore, shall Zion (the spiritual point from which reality emerges) rise to the top—for your sake, be plowed like a field (clearing the hay) and the old kingdom will become heaps of hay and the physical body (tent, temple, house—where the soul resides) will be the high place in the forest where we will all be able to see with a new set of eyes. It is time, time to let go of the old and move into the new.

## *In the Beginning God Created Heaven and Earth*

Now the work begins with each of God's children—each God-soul using their oil and seed (our will, making a soul choice) to create manna for the feast (manifest) for your life (tree of life). Only God's children can create their daily bread (manna) because God the Creator created the seeds and gave them oil. ☺

You choose—no one can choose for you, and you cannot choose for anyone else. You cannot force feed the manna, and you cannot be forced to eat the manna by anyone or anything. It may not be your time or your purpose yet—the soul knows.

Some of us will stay to hold the fort down in the old kingdom, while others will climb up the stairway to heaven and hold the door open for the others. Don't worry because worry and fear will hold you back—olive (all of) us will come one by one and olive us will unite as "ONE" when the work is done.

Whenever "olive" us create something new like a house, temple, kingdom or a "New Earth", some souls have to stay back to take care of the old dwellings until the new one is in operation and the old one is no longer needed. Honor and be thankful for "olive" thy neighbors, thy family, thy friends and thy enemies, too. Please understand why things had to be the way they were—pure unconditional love is what makes the cosmos go round and round. Each soul has a divine purpose—each with a divine plan that has been masterfully planned by "olive" us collectively.

Once you mix your "oil" with the seeds (grain), you will make manna. Consume the manna for energy to start your long journey home and climb Jacob's Ladder, the "Stairway to Heaven on Earth" to find the Holy Book (Holy Grail).

As you go through the pages one by one—reviewing, changing, removing old beliefs, old systems, old words and pages of the past within your "Holy Book"—you the "Great Invisible Spirit" will come to terms and discover "The Kingdom of Heaven", paradise on the New Earth. And so it is . . .

## *THE BEGINNING . . .*

**Genesis 1 (KJV)**
*[1]In the beginning God created the heaven and the earth. [2]And the earth was without form, and void; and darkness was upon the face of the deep. And the Spirit of God moved upon the face of the waters. [3]And God said, Let there be light: and there was light. [4]And God saw the light, that it was good: and God divided the light from the darkness. [5]And God called the light Day, and the darkness he called Night. And the evening and the morning were the first day.*

*[6]And God said, Let there be a firmament in the midst of the waters, and let it divide the waters from the waters. [7]And God made the firmament, and divided the waters which were under the firmament from the waters which were above the firmament: and it was so. [8]And God called the firmament Heaven. And the evening and the morning were the second day.*

*[9]And God said, Let the waters under the heaven be gathered together unto one place, and let the dry land appear: and it was so. [10]And God called the dry land Earth; and the gathering together of the waters called he Seas: and God saw that it was good. [11]And God said, Let the earth bring forth grass, the herb yielding seed, and the fruit tree yielding fruit after his kind, whose seed is in itself, upon the earth: and it was so.*

*[12]And the earth brought forth grass, and herb yielding seed after his kind, and the tree yielding fruit, whose seed was in itself, after his kind: and God saw that it was good. [13]And the evening and the morning were the third day. [14]And God said, Let there be lights in the firmament of the heaven to divide the day from the night; and let them be for signs, and for seasons, and for days, and years: [15]And let them be for lights in the firmament of the heaven to give light upon the earth: and it was so.*

¹⁶And God made two great lights; the greater light to rule the day, and the lesser light to rule the night: he made the stars also. ¹⁷And God set them in the firmament of the heaven to give light upon the earth, ¹⁸And to rule over the day and over the night, and to divide the light from the darkness: and God saw that it was good. ¹⁹And the evening and the morning were the fourth day.

²⁰And God said, Let the waters bring forth abundantly the moving creature that hath life, and fowl that may fly above the earth in the open firmament of heaven. ²¹And God created great whales, and every living creature that moveth, which the waters brought forth abundantly, after their kind, and every winged fowl after his kind: and God saw that it was good. ²²And God blessed them, saying, Be fruitful, and multiply, and fill the waters in the seas, and let fowl multiply in the earth. ²³And the evening and the morning were the fifth day.

²⁴And God said, Let the earth bring forth the living creature after his kind, cattle, and creeping thing, and beast of the earth after his kind: and it was so. ²⁵And God made the beast of the earth after his kind, and cattle after their kind, and every thing that creepeth upon the earth after his kind: and God saw that it was good. ²⁶And God said, Let us make man in our image, after our likeness: and let them have dominion over the fish of the sea, and over the fowl of the air, and over the cattle, and over all the earth, and over every creeping thing that creepeth upon the earth.

²⁷So God created man in his own image, in the image of God created he him; male and female created he them. ²⁸And God blessed them, and God said unto them, Be fruitful, and multiply, and replenish the earth, and subdue it: and have dominion over the fish of the sea, and over the fowl of the air, and over every living thing that moveth upon the earth. ²⁹And God said, Behold, I have given you every herb bearing seed, which is upon the face of all the earth, and every tree, in them which is the fruit of a tree yielding seed; to you it shall be for meat.

³⁰And to every beast of the earth, and to every fowl of the air, and to every thing that creepeth upon the earth, wherein there is life, I have given every green herb for meat: and it was so. ³¹And God saw every

*thing that he had made, and, behold, it was very good. And the evening and the morning were the sixth day.* THE BEGINNING

## IT ALL BEGINS WITH YOU ☺

## AWAKEN THE SLEEPING GIANT within

## SANETHA's HEALING SOUL-U-TIONS www.sanetha.com

*visit the website for additional information and to add your questions and comments regarding the book.

### SANETHA'S SOULGENIC (ANGELIC) HEALING and Presentations

I am a spiritual clairsentient healer and interpreter who brought these gifts and abilities with me in my DNA since the time of Lemuria. I access frequencies at the soul level (all of your lifetimes) therefore healing occurs on a multidimensional level bringing light and information to all of your physical, mental, emotional and spiritual bodies.

Over your lifetimes you have created experiences both good and bad with one soul purpose in mind—How to get back home again. When you arrived in this life, you brought with you karma that may have you enduring hardships and/or illness. The end of those days have arrived and you no longer need to suffer needlessly. The time is NOW to let go of the baggage that is holding you back and reclaim your birth rights.

I have access to the new energy available now here on the new earth for the very first time! Discover your path to your awakening to know Who you are, Where you came from, How you got here AND How to get back home again.

Heal all of you from inside out! Your personal guides and angels will be present during all of your sessions. "OIL" is required for "oliive" us to gain the desired results.

***SANETHA'S THREE DAYS AND THREE NIGHTS SOULGENIC HEALING RETREAT—connect with me through the website for a retreat near you or create one of your own in your area.***

*SAATCH—Spiritual Awareness, Acceptance, Transformation and Change*

1) AWARENESS—Becoming familiar with your spiritual self

2) ACCEPTANCE—Your intention to move forward on your spiritual path

3) TRANSFORMATION—The process of "clearing the hay" to reconnect with your divine blueprint

4) CHANGING YOUR DNA

Printed in Great Britain
by Amazon